S. Hrg. 114–269

ZERO STARS: HOW GAGGING HONEST REVIEWS HARMS CONSUMERS AND THE ECONOMY

HEARING

BEFORE THE

COMMITTEE ON COMMERCE, SCIENCE, AND TRANSPORTATION UNITED STATES SENATE

ONE HUNDRED FOURTEENTH CONGRESS

FIRST SESSION

NOVEMBER 4, 2015

Printed for the use of the Committee on Commerce, Science, and Transportation

U.S. GOVERNMENT PUBLISHING OFFICE

20–128 PDF　　　　WASHINGTON : 2016

For sale by the Superintendent of Documents, U.S. Government Publishing Office
Internet: bookstore.gpo.gov　Phone: toll free (866) 512–1800; DC area (202) 512–1800
Fax: (202) 512–2104　Mail: Stop IDCC, Washington, DC 20402–0001

SENATE COMMITTEE ON COMMERCE, SCIENCE, AND TRANSPORTATION

ONE HUNDRED FOURTEENTH CONGRESS

FIRST SESSION

JOHN THUNE, South Dakota, *Chairman*

ROGER F. WICKER, Mississippi	BILL NELSON, Florida, *Ranking*
ROY BLUNT, Missouri	MARIA CANTWELL, Washington
MARCO RUBIO, Florida	CLAIRE McCASKILL, Missouri
KELLY AYOTTE, New Hampshire	AMY KLOBUCHAR, Minnesota
TED CRUZ, Texas	RICHARD BLUMENTHAL, Connecticut
DEB FISCHER, Nebraska	BRIAN SCHATZ, Hawaii
JERRY MORAN, Kansas	EDWARD MARKEY, Massachusetts
DAN SULLIVAN, Alaska	CORY BOOKER, New Jersey
RON JOHNSON, Wisconsin	TOM UDALL, New Mexico
DEAN HELLER, Nevada	JOE MANCHIN III, West Virginia
CORY GARDNER, Colorado	GARY PETERS, Michigan
STEVE DAINES, Montana	

DAVID SCHWIETERT, *Staff Director*
NICK ROSSI, *Deputy Staff Director*
REBECCA SEIDEL, *General Counsel*
JASON VAN BEEK, *Deputy General Counsel*
KIM LIPSKY, *Democratic Staff Director*
CHRIS DAY, *Democratic Deputy Staff Director*
CLINT ODOM, *Democratic General Counsel and Policy Director*

CONTENTS

	Page
Hearing held on November 4, 2015	1
Statement of Senator Thune	1
Statement of Senator Nelson	3
Statement of Senator McCaskill	44
Statement of Senator Fischer	46
Statement of Senator Moran	48
Statement of Senator Schatz	50
Statement of Senator Daines	51
Statement of Senator Klobuchar	54
Statement of Senator Blumenthal	56
Statement of Senator Markey	57

WITNESSES

	Page
Adam Medros, Senior Vice President, Head of Global Product, TripAdvisor LLC	5
Prepared statement	7
Robert Atkinson, President, Information Technology and Innovation Foundation	9
Prepared statement of Daniel Castro, Vice President, Information Technology and Innovation Foundation	10
Jennifer Kulas Palmer, Plaintiff, Palmer v. KlearGear	14
Prepared statement	16
Eric Goldman, Professor, Santa Clara University School of Law	18
Prepared statement	20
Article dated November 2, 2015 entitled "How Congress Can Protect Online Consumer Reviews"	21
Article dated March 27, 2015 entitled "Court Might Enforce A Contract Ban On Consumer Reviews"	23
Article dated September 10, 2014 entitled "California Tells Businesses: Stop Trying To Ban Consumer Reviews"	23
Article dated August 7, 2014 entitled "Fining Customers For Negative Online Reviews Isn't New...Or Smart	24
Article from The Next Digital Decade:Essays on the Future of the Internet entitled "The Regulation of Reputational Information"	28
Article from *Medical Ethics* entitled "Patients' Online Reviews of Physicians"	34
Ira Rheingold, Executive Director, National Association of Consumer Advocates	35
Prepared statement	37

APPENDIX

	Page
Scott Michelman, Staff Attorney, Public Citizen, prepared statement	63
Angie Hicks, Founder and Chief Marketing Officer, Angie's List, prepared statement	67
Letter dated November 3, 2015 to Hon. John Thune and Hon. Bill Nelson from George P. Slover, Senior Policy Counsel, Consumers Union	68
Letter dated November 4, 2015 to Hon. John Thune and Hon. Bill Nelson from Mike Godwin, R Street Institute; Mytheos Holt, Institute for Liberty; and Steve Pociask, American Consumer Institute	69
Letter dated November 4, 2015 to Hon. John Thune and Hon. Bill Nelson from Michael Beckerman, President and CEO, The Internet Association	70

	Page
Letter dated November 3, 2015 to Chairman Thune and Ranking Member Nelson from the companies: Demand Progress, Engine, Electronic Frontier Foundation, Fight for the Future, Glassdoor, Information Technology & Innovation Foundation (ITIF), Public Knowledge, Public Participation Project, RealSelf, R Street and Yelp	71
Letter dated November 3, 2015 from Chi Chi Wu, National Consumer Law Center (on behalf of its low-income clients)	72

ZERO STARS: HOW GAGGING HONEST REVIEWS HARMS CONSUMERS AND THE ECONOMY

WEDNESDAY, NOVEMBER 4, 2015

U.S. SENATE,
COMMITTEE ON COMMERCE, SCIENCE, AND TRANSPORTATION,
Washington, DC.

The Committee met, pursuant to notice, at 10:02 a.m., in room SR–253, Russell Senate Office Building, Hon. John Thune, Chairman of the Committee, presiding.

Present: Senators Thune [presiding], Blunt, Ayotte, Fischer, Moran, Gardner, Daines, Nelson, Cantwell, McCaskill, Klobuchar, Blumenthal, Schatz, Markey, and Manchin.

OPENING STATEMENT OF HON. JOHN THUNE, U.S. SENATOR FROM SOUTH DAKOTA

The CHAIRMAN. Good morning. This hearing will come to order.

Today, we convene to examine a growing and disturbing trend affecting consumers in the United States.

Imagine you are a consumer who purchases an item online, but the product isn't what you bargained for. Because you don't want other consumers to waste their time or money, you take to social media to post an honest account of your experience. You are then aggressively approached by the company that sold you the substandard product and threatened with a stiff penalty unless you immediately take down the critical review.

Little did you know that buried in the fine print of the website's terms and conditions was an anti-consumer clause forbidding you from posting a negative review about the company, even if it is true. This scenario sounds farfetched, but the sad reality is that it is happening every day across the country.

So-called non-disparagement or gag clauses are being forced on consumers and then being used to intimidate them. These gag provisions are egregious from a consumer protection standpoint, but they are also doing harm to our Internet ecosystem.

Our committee spends a significant amount of time focusing on how we can increase broadband adoption and create policies that unlock the true potential of the Internet, but speech-stifling contract terms undermine what we are trying to accomplish in Internet policy.

A core tenet of the Internet is the ability to freely share information with whomever you like. What good is information if it has been sanitized to remove truthful criticism?

Simply put, imposing consumer gag clauses can result in unfair bullying. The practice is frequently about a larger entity abusing its power and insulating itself from legitimate and constructive criticism.

Often, consumers don't believe they have any power against companies that treat them poorly, but online review sites and social media have given American consumers a tremendous amount of power. Consumers rightfully place high value on the experiences of other consumers and therefore frequently rely on the wisdom of the crowd when deciding where to spend their money.

Do some consumers sometimes abuse the Internet with false reviews? Sure, they do. But businesses that face unfair reviews have existing remedies available to them, including the ability to sue for defamation. In addition, businesses should be able to offset phony reviews with positive assessments from satisfied customers.

Regrettably, there are a growing number of businesses in the marketplace that are blocking honest consumer speech through gag clauses rather than responding to negative criticism by providing a better product or service.

Today, we are joined by Jen Palmer, who will share her personal experience fighting against an unscrupulous company that sought a $3,500 penalty simply because she told the truth about poor customer service. Fortunately for the Palmers, they were able to challenge this abuse in court and persevered.

The Palmers are far from alone in their experience. In one case, a dentist included a non-disparagement clause in her contract, as well as a clause that purported to grant the dentist the copyright to anything the patient may later write about the dentist. When a patient posted an online review complaining about being overcharged, the dentist sent a take-down notice to the review site. The dentist also sent the patient a series of invoices demanding payment of $100 for each day the complaints continued to appear online. The patient sued the dentist, and a court found the clause to be unconscionable and void, awarding the patient nearly $5,000.

In another case, a consumer who did not receive her order from an online retailer informed the company she would report the matter to her credit card company. In response, the company demanded the consumer pay $250 for violation of its fine-print terms of sale, which prohibited a customer from even threatening to make a negative public statement about the retailer. The consumer filed suit against the retailer, alleging its actions were unfair, deceptive, and contrary to public policy, and the court ultimately found in the consumer's favor.

Going even a step further, in a wedding contract, one hotel went so far as to inform prospective newlyweds they could be fined if they or any of their guests violated a gag clause by leaving a negative review. After this clause was reported widely in the press, the business changed its terms.

Keep in mind, the vast majority of non-disparagement clauses never see public light. This is because consumers often succumb to pressure and remove the negative review. Understandably, they would rather avoid the fight than face the threat of excessive penalties, costly litigation, or damage to their credit scores.

The proliferation of this problem led Senators Moran, Schatz, Blumenthal, McCaskill, and me to introduce the bipartisan and bicameral Consumer Review Freedom Act that would ban non-disparagement clauses in form contracts while still permitting companies to pursue good faith defamation claims.

Our bill empowers the Federal Trade Commission and State Attorneys General to enforce against these anti-consumer provisions. The FTC recently filed suit against one company over a consumer gag clause, and the Consumer Review Freedom Act would guarantee the Commission's ability to fight against these provisions.

Since introduction, we have worked with stakeholders and plan to make a few changes prior to marking up the bill. I am looking forward to moving this pro-consumer legislation through our committee and the Senate so Americans can continue to help each other make informed decisions.

We have an excellent panel here today with diverse experiences on this issue. You each bring a unique perspective, and I look forward to hearing about your experiences and thoughts on our legislation. So I want to thank you for agreeing to testify and to be with us today.

Senator Nelson?

STATEMENT OF HON. BILL NELSON,
U.S. SENATOR FROM FLORIDA

Senator NELSON. Thank you, Mr. Chairman.

So companies want to muzzle consumers, and these companies are using their size and unequal bargaining power to force consumers to sign these take-it-or-leave-it agreements or contracts.

In some cases, these agreements are just online pop-up items that a consumer clicks on, usually without reading all the small print, to purchase a good or service on the Internet. Almost no one reads them, but they can have major consequences.

Now, when I was in law school, they called these "contracts of adhesion." They are called "adhesion" because you are stuck with them. You can't modify the contract in any way. You are bound by the fine print that lawyers are so good at drafting.

And the idea that some companies are suing or threatening to sue their customers for truthfully reviewing their consumer experiences because of these so-called non-disparagement clauses in contracts in the fine print, I think it is appalling.

So we need to do something about it. And, thankfully, Mr. Chairman, you are.

In a state like mine, Florida that is so dependent on tourism, we want visitors to share their experiences. Businesses that do a good job should be rewarded with good comments, and those who do not, they ought to be punished by telling the truth.

So, Mr. Chairman, I am glad that your bill would stop this practice by voiding contracts of adhesion that punish consumers for sharing their experiences and their opinions with other consumers.

Now, I think this hearing is timely, Mr. Chairman, because this issue and your bill brings up, in my mind, a related issue that needs to be discussed. Just a few weeks ago, the *Los Angeles Times* reported that Fiat Chrysler was requiring consumers who wanted to receive a family discount on a car to sign a mandatory arbitration clause as part of the sales contract.

So if the car is defective and kills or injures that consumer, as was the case with Toyota's sudden acceleration or GM's faulty ignition switches or Takata's exploding airbags, then you are potentially barred from seeking redress because of that take-it-or-leave-it arbitration clause. This type of provision is obviously outrageous.

And beyond the automakers themselves, many dealers are also trying to use these arbitration provisions to shield themselves.

This committee has seen too many examples lately of companies getting away scot-free for killing and injuring and hiding the truth. And these non-disparagement and arbitration clauses are just another way for companies to avoid accountability by silencing consumers.

So, yes, consumers ought to be able to write a negative review about their business experience, but consumers should also have the ability to seek justice in a court of law when businesses fail to hold up their end of the bargain, especially if that failure ends up in injury or death. We just simply can't let people continue to get off scot-free.

So thank you, Mr. Chairman. Thank you for the hearing.

The CHAIRMAN. Thank you, Senator Nelson, for those comments.

And I want to, for the record, just add a couple of letters of support for the legislation.

This one is from Angie Hicks of Angie's List, in which she says, "The bipartisan Consumer Review Freedom Act would prohibit the use of these clauses, agreements, and waivers, which are blatant though often cleverly disguised efforts to strip Americans of their right to honestly discuss their service experience."

The Internet Association says, "We applaud today's hearing on the bill," a bipartisan bill introduced, as I mentioned, by several of our colleagues.

American Consumer Institute: Center for Citizen Research, R Street, and the Institute for Liberty, also a letter of support.

And then one, as well, from another coalition that includes Yelp, Public Knowledge, Public Participation Project, RealSelf, among many others.

So I want to enter those for the record.

[Please see Appendix for these letters.]

The CHAIRMAN. And I now want to open it up, and look forward to hearing from our panel today.

We have with us, beginning on my left, Mr. Adam Medros, who is the Senior Vice President for Global Product at TripAdvisor; Mr. Robert Atkinson, who is the President of the Information Technology and Innovation Foundation; Ms. Jennifer Palmer, who I mentioned earlier is one of the named plaintiffs in *Palmer* v. *KlearGear;* Mr. Eric Goldman is a Professor at Santa Clara University of Law and is also the Director of the school's High Tech Law Institute; and then, finally, Mr. Ira Rheingold, who is the Executive Director of the National Association of Consumer Advocates.

So welcome to all of you. Great to have you here today.

And we will start on my left and your right with Mr. Medros, and please proceed with your statement. If you could, confine it as close to 5 minutes as possible, and then we will get into some questions here from the panel.

STATEMENT OF ADAM MEDROS, SENIOR VICE PRESIDENT, HEAD OF GLOBAL PRODUCT, TRIPADVISOR LLC

Mr. MEDROS. Good morning, Chairman Thune, Ranking Member Nelson, and members of the Commerce Committee. Thank you for inviting me to testify in today's hearing on what we believe is a very important topic. I am encouraged by the Committee's attention to this issue and very much appreciate your recent introduction of the Consumer Review Freedom Act.

My name is Adam Medros. I am the Head of Global Product for TripAdvisor, the world's largest travel website. I lead the team within TripAdvisor that is responsible for all customer-facing aspects of the TripAdvisor site, including the collection, moderation, and display of travelers' reviews.

For those who don't recall what it was like to plan and book a trip prior to the advent of the Internet, let's rewind 15 years.

Making travel purchases, because of their significant costs, the infrequent nature of travel, and the importance that we place on vacations, was a risky proposition. You either had to research and plan the trip on your own, calling multiple hotels and airlines to check availability and pricing, or rely on a travel agent looking up brochures filled with marketing language and staged photographs. If you were really lucky, maybe a friend had visited that city or country before. But to put it simply, you were buying blind.

The Internet and platforms like TripAdvisor drastically improved that experience for consumers. With access to millions of customer reviews, our ability to make informed purchasing decisions is no longer constrained to what products our friends and family purchased or where one's local travel agent thinks you should stay on vacation.

As a result, American consumers can make significantly more informed decisions about how to spend their hard-earned money.

Although most businesses have come to embrace this shift in consumers' knowledge, a minority of holdouts refuse to let consumers share their experiences. A popular tactic among such businesses is to try and use their contractual leverage to silence their critics. This underhanded practice harms those writing reviews, those seeking transparency through other consumers' experiences, and those businesses that are playing by the rules.

TripAdvisor hosts more than 250 million reviews and opinions from our community, covering more than 5 million businesses all over the world. TripAdvisor encourages our members to share their reviews and opinions, good or bad, of their experiences at hotels, restaurants, and attractions, and we strongly believe in their right to do so.

We also give all businesses the right to respond to those reviews in order to ensure that consumers are presented with both sides of the story.

As you know, TripAdvisor is far from the only source of consumer reviews. Americans are ever-increasingly turning to websites like Amazon, Yelp, ZocDoc, and Angie's List to educate themselves in their purchasing decisions on everything from what doctor to visit to whom they should hire to remodel their kitchens. In fact, a recent study revealed that approximately 70 percent of all American shoppers rely on online reviews before making a purchase.

Just this year, the United Kingdom's Competition and Markets Authority found that 54 percent of U.K. adults rely upon online reviews and that nearly 70 percent of hotel shoppers consider online reviews to be more important than other sources of information.

No matter what population is being researched, it is clear that consumer reviews have become a critical part of today's marketplace.

While consumer reviews have become so ubiquitous that many Americans won't make a significant buying decision without first researching those opinions, we know that some businesses don't like the transparency that online reviews have brought to the world.

Some bully or intimidate consumers as a means to get critical reviews removed or to stop them from even being submitted. Others seek the same result by hiding small print in contracts stipulating that any negative review will incur a hefty fine or assigning the intellectual property in any review to the business.

Consumers usually have no idea that they are signing up for such agreements, which are usually only provided in small print at the moment of check-in or purchase. And even those who actually read these types of clauses lack the leverage to have the non-negotiable clauses removed while standing at the check-in desk with their family in tow and their well-earned vacation hanging in the balance.

While the intention behind such clauses is always the same—namely, to gag any negative opinions—the exact language can vary. Examples of language that TripAdvisor has received from travelers include: "Since bad reviews are detrimental to our business, we place a fine for unwarranted reviews under the terms of property. If the hotel receives a poor review and is out of context and or control of the hotel management, then a fine of $300 will be charged on the credit card on file."

Dealing with companies and individuals that try to include these types of clauses in their customer agreements can be tricky for a platform like TripAdvisor. While the easiest solution would be to simply remove the business's listing from our website, that is often exactly what the company wants: to eliminate the ability for consumers to comment on them. Doing so would chill speech and be a disservice to all travelers.

So TripAdvisor has instead taken the approach of posting a red text box on the business's listing warning travelers of this unscrupulous behavior. This is an imperfect solution and one which would be improved upon by passage of Chairman Thune's Consumer Review Freedom Act.

Placing a muzzle on one's customers with contractual boilerplate goes against everything we stand for at TripAdvisor. Just as a consumer can tell her family and friends about her experience with a business in the "offline world," she also has a right to share that experience and opinion online, allowing businesses and other customers to learn and benefit therefrom.

When a business includes a ''gag order'' in its agreements with its customers, everyone is harmed. The consumer is improperly censored. The consuming public at large is less informed than it otherwise would be about quality of service, or lack thereof, at a given business. Even the business doing the silencing is harmed, as it loses the opportunity to learn from the experiences of its customers.

These types of clauses serve no positive role in the American marketplace and stand in the way of consumer transparency.

In conclusion, Mr. Chairman, TripAdvisor looks forward to working with you and the entire committee to ensure that American consumers are not prevented from openly sharing their opinions and experiences with other potential customers, whether it is done in person or via the Internet.

I welcome your questions on this important topic.

[The prepared statement of Mr. Medros follows:]

PREPARED STATEMENT OF ADAM MEDROS, SENIOR VICE PRESIDENT, HEAD OF GLOBAL PRODUCT, TRIPADVISOR LLC

Good morning Chairman Thune, Ranking Member Nelson, and members of the Commerce Committee. Thank you for inviting me to testify in today's hearing on what we believe is a very important topic. I am encouraged by the Committee's attention on this issue, and very much appreciate your recent introduction of the *Consumer Review Freedom Act.*

I. Introduction

My name is Adam Medros, and I am the Head of Global Product for TripAdvisor, the world's largest travel website. I lead the team within TripAdvisor that is responsible for all customer-facing aspects of the TripAdvisor site, including the collection, moderation and display of travelers' reviews.

For those who don't recall what it was like to plan and book travel prior to the advent of the Internet, let's pause and rewind fifteen years. Making travel purchases—because of their significant cost, the infrequent nature of travel and the importance that we place on vacations—was a risky proposition. You either had to research and plan the trip on your own, calling multiple hotels and airlines to check availability and pricing, or rely on a travel agent discussing destinations they chose to promote and looking at brochures filled with marketing language and staged photographs. If you were really lucky, maybe a friend or family member had visited that city or country before, and could give you an opinion based on their limited experiences. But to put it simply, you were ''buying blind.''

The Internet—and platforms like TripAdvisor—drastically improved that experience for consumers. With access to millions of consumer reviews in seconds, our ability to make informed purchasing decisions is no longer constrained to what products our friends and family previously purchased, or where one's local travel agent thinks you should stay on vacation. As a result, American consumers can make significantly more informed decisions about how to spend their hard-earned money. Platforms like ours democratized purchasing and access to information by crowdsourcing the experiences of others.

However, although most businesses have come to accept—and even embrace—this shift in consumers' knowledge, a minority of hold-outs refuse to let consumers share their experiences. A popular tactic among such businesses is to try and use their contractual leverage to silence their critics. This underhanded practice harms those writing reviews, those seeking transparency through other consumers' experiences, and those businesses that are playing by the rules, and, ultimately, the American economy suffers.

II. TripAdvisor and The Importance of Consumer Reviews

TripAdvisor is visited by more than 375 million travelers a month in order to help them research, plan and book the perfect trip. We host more than 250 million reviews and opinions from our community covering more than 5 million businesses all over the world. TripAdvisor encourages our members to share their reviews and opinions, good or bad, of their experiences at hotels, restaurants, and attractions—and we strongly believe in their right to do so. We also give all businesses the right to respond to those reviews, in order to ensure that consumers are presented with both sides of the story.

As you know, TripAdvisor is far from the only source of consumer reviews. Americans are ever-increasingly turning to websites like Yelp, Amazon, ZocDoc and Angie's List to educate themselves and their purchasing decisions on everything from what doctor to visit, to what book or baby stroller to purchase, or even to whom they should hire to remodel their kitchens. In fact, a recent study revealed that approximately 70 percent of all American shoppers rely on online reviews before making a purchase.[1] Just this year, the United Kingdom's Competition and Markets Authority found that 54 percent of UK adults rely upon online reviews, and that nearly 70 percent of hotel shoppers consider online reviews to be more important than other sources of information. Further, in research commissioned by TripAdvisor in 2015, PhoCusWright determined that 96 percent of TripAdvisor users consider it important to read consumer reviews when planning a vacation, and 82 percent agreed that reading those reviews helped them plan better trips than they could without reviews. No matter what population is being researched, it is clear that consumer reviews have become a critical part of today's marketplace.

III. Businesses' Use of Contracts to Silence Critics

While consumer reviews have become so ubiquitous that many Americans won't make a significant buying decision without first researching those opinions, we know that some businesses don't like the transparency that online reviews have brought to the world. Some bully or intimidate consumers as a means to get critical reviews removed or to stop them from even being submitted. Others seek the same result by hiding small print in contracts stipulating that any negative reviews will incur a hefty fine, or assigning the intellectual property in any review to the business.

Consumers usually have no idea that they are signing-up for such agreements, which are usually only provided in small print at the moment of check-in or purchase, and even those who actually read these types of clauses lack the leverage to have the non-negotiable clauses removed while standing at the check-in desk with their family in tow and their well-earned vacation hanging in the balance. While the intent behind such clauses is always the same (namely, to gag any negative opinions), the exact language can vary. Examples of language that TripAdvisor has received from travelers include:

> "Guest agrees that no negative comment will ever be initiated . . . on any site on the Internet . . . that damages the reputation of the hotel and staff . . . ."

> "Since bad reviews are detrimental to our business, we place a fine for unwarranted reviews under the terms of property . . . [I]f the hotel receives a poor review and is out of context and or control of the hotel management, then a fine of $300 will be charged on the credit card on file."

> "[I] any actual opinions and/or publications are created which, at the sole opinion of [business owner], tends directly to injure him in respect to his trade or business . . . then those remarks will entitle [business owner] . . . damages from me in the amount of $5,000,000 (five million dollars) plus a $50,000 (fifty-thousand dollar) daily penalty for each day for each posting of the derogatory publication appears or is available in any format."

Dealing with companies and individuals that try to include these types of clauses in their customer agreements can be tricky for a platform like TripAdvisor. While the easiest solution would be to simply remove the business's listing from our website, that is often exactly what that company *wants*—to eliminate the ability for consumers to comment on them. Doing so would chill speech and be a disservice to all travelers, so TripAdvisor has instead taken the approach of posting a red text box on the business's listing warning travelers of this unscrupulous practice. This is an imperfect solution—and one which would be improved upon by passage of Chairman Thune's *Consumer Review Freedom Act*.

IV. The Effects Chilled Speech Has on Industry and Consumers

Placing a muzzle on one's customers with contractual boilerplate goes against everything we stand for at TripAdvisor. Just as a consumer can tell her friends and family about her experience with a business in the "offline world," she also has a right to share that experience and opinion online, allowing businesses and other customers to learn and benefit therefrom.

---

[1] The Consumerist (Jun. 3, 2015), *http://consumerist.com/2015/06/03/nearly-70-of-consu mers-rely-on-online-reviews-before-making-a-purchase/*; Ashlee Kieler, *Nearly 70% Of Consumers Rely On Online Reviews Before Making A Purchase.*

When a business includes a ''gag order'' in its agreements with its customers, everyone is harmed. The consumer is improperly censored. The consuming public at-large is less informed than it otherwise would be about the quality of service—or lack thereof—at a given business. Even the business doing the silencing is harmed, as it loses the opportunity to learn from the experiences of its customers. These types of clauses serve no positive role in the American marketplace and stand in the way of consumer transparency.

V. Conclusion

In conclusion, Mr. Chairman, TripAdvisor looks forward to working with you and the entire Committee to ensure that American consumers are not prevented from openly sharing their opinions and experiences with other potential customers, whether it is done in-person or via the Internet.

I welcome your questions on this important topic.

The CHAIRMAN. Thank you, Mr. Medros.

Mr. Atkinson?

STATEMENT OF ROBERT ATKINSON, PRESIDENT, INFORMATION TECHNOLOGY AND INNOVATION FOUNDATION

Mr. ATKINSON. Thank you, Chairman Thune, Ranking Member Nelson, and members of the Committee. I appreciate the opportunity to come before you today to talk about the impact of non-disparagement clauses on consumers and the economy.

The Information Technology and Innovation Foundation has long focused on policies to enable the Internet economy to thrive, and this particular area that you are addressing with the Consumer Review Freedom Act is a critical one if that is going to be our goal.

I want to raise three issues today, the first one really being about economy theory and economics behind this.

There has long been a view in economics that the effective functioning of markets depends upon information. In fact, George Akerlof, Michael Spence, and Joe Stiglitz received the Nobel Prize in economics in 2001 for their research related to what they called ''asymmetric information,'' and this is exactly what is going on here. When you go to a hotel, you don't know anything about the hotel other than maybe what you see; the hotel knows everything. This is a market with asymmetric information.

And they won that prize because they showed that markets with asymmetric information underperform what would be otherwise economic welfare for everyone—consumers and the overall economy.

And, in particular, this and other economics research has found that markets don't perform effectively if, number one, buyers can't accurately assess the value of the product or service before they buy it. If you go to a hotel and you have no idea what is going on there, you can't make an informed decision.

Second, if an incentive exists for the seller to pass off a low-quality product or service as a high-quality one, well, clearly, as the examples have shown, that incentive exists certainly for some sellers.

Third, where the sellers of good products and services have a hard time proving their quality.

And, fourth, where there is a deficiency of public quality assurances—in others words, where it is hard for a consumer to find some independent assessments of quality.

That is why the emergence of online rating tools are so important. They essentially are the tool to solve this long, age-old problem that has bedeviled economic markets. And online rating systems help solve the problem because they provide a public quality assurance of that, and they let people know why and when there is poor quality.

The second point is the issue about preemption. I know that some argue that the Federal Government shouldn't be involved in some of these questions and we should just let the states deal with these questions and they are better positioned for that.

And, certainly, on many, many issues, in many cases, states are best-positioned. But, in general, when it comes to the Internet economy, we can't rely on states to set policies for two big reasons.

One is that you end up with a cacophony of different and conflicting policies between states. And the second reason is that, in many of these cases—TripAdvisor hotel reviews in Florida, many of those are non-Florida residents. So a state might say, well, we want to protect our businesses by not allowing this, but they are hurting consumers all around the country because consumers everywhere use these and contribute to these.

So I think it really is a very clear justification for Federal action.

The third would be, well, what about the possible harms to businesses where there is a bad review? And I think it has been pointed out already that this bill would not prohibit companies from already using existing legal tools for defamation.

But, more importantly, there has been a lot of evidence now that we cite in our testimony that, even when a company receives a bad review, if the company manager, whoever that might be, affirmatively responds to that review and says, "We are sorry," or, "Thanks for the review; we are going to try to fix that problem," it actually turns out that that gets them better results with consumers because consumers believe that the manager or the company is taking consumer complaints seriously and so they are more likely to trust them.

This was a study, for example, recently about hotels, and found that, regardless of whether reviews are good, neutral, or negative, they began to receive higher ratings from guests after hotel managers started to respond to feedback. And I have heard that from hotel managers when we have done some study on hotels. They actively go out now and tell the managers that they should respond online because it brings back trust.

So I don't think we should worry too much about the impact on companies. If companies are smart, what they will do will be they will affirmatively monitor these ratings platforms and then respond appropriately. Where there are clear cases of defamation and outright lies, again, they have other legal means.

So, in summary, that is why ITF supports this legislation and believes it is very important for the online marketplace.

Thank you.

[The prepared statement of Mr. Daniel Castro, submitted by Mr. Atkinson, follows:]

PREPARED STATEMENT OF DANIEL CASTRO, VICE PRESIDENT, INFORMATION TECHNOLOGY AND INNOVATION FOUNDATION

Chairman Thune, Ranking Member Nelson, and members of the Committee, I appreciate the opportunity to appear before you to discuss the impact of non-disparagement clauses on consumers and businesses. My name is Daniel Castro. I am the Vice President of the Information Technology and Innovation Foundation (ITIF) and Director of ITIF's Center for Data Innovation. ITIF is a nonpartisan, non-profit think tank whose mission is to formulate and promote policy solutions that accelerate innovation and boost productivity to spur growth, opportunity, and progress.

In my testimony today, I would like to discuss how the non-disparagement clauses that many businesses include in consumer contracts discourage consumers from providing honest feedback about products and services; why that harms consumers and businesses alike; and what Congress can do to address the problem.

Some Businesses Use Non-Disparagement Clauses to Unfairly Silence Critics

Imagine that a patient has endured a terrible visit to the dentist. Disturbed by the ordeal, she goes online and posts a review, providing a factual account of her experience as a warning to future patients. Soon after, the patient receives a letter from the dentist's lawyer stating that she is in violation of a contract she signed during her visit and threatening legal action if she does not immediately take down the post. Shockingly, she discovers that buried in the paperwork she filled out was a clause prohibiting her from making any negative statements about the dentist. Scared that she may have done something wrong, and worried about the cost of going to court, the patient quickly deletes her review. Not only has this patient had her voice unfairly silenced, but many other potential patients will not be able to benefit from her experience by choosing a better dentist.

This scenario is one that an untold number of consumers have faced. A company will insert a clause into a standard contract that prohibits consumers from making any negative statements about the company and its products or services. Most consumers sign these agreements without noticing the non-disparagement clauses. Only later, if at all, do they ever realize what they have agreed to. For example, health care providers may ask patients to sign "mutual privacy agreements" that are less about protecting patient privacy (since Federal laws already provide these protections), but instead are designed to prohibit patients from making negative comments about the health care provider.[1] Alternatively, a company may demand that an unhappy customer sign a non-disparagement agreement before the company will provide a refund or exchange.[2] In both cases, companies may sue consumers for monetary damages if they subsequently make negative public comments about their products or services.

While there are no good estimates of how many consumers have been silenced by these non-disparagement clauses or how many companies regularly insert these clauses into their contracts, there are many well-documented cases of this problem arising in a variety of industries, including health care, retail, and hospitality. For example, one party rental company included the following terms in its standard contract: "By signing this contract, you are agreeing that you will not make or encourage any disparaging comments about [the vendor] ever in any form verbal or written."[3]

These non-disparagement clauses are particularly problematic because they are appearing in non-negotiated consumer contracts and even website terms of service without giving consumers a reasonable opportunity to negotiate or refuse to accept the conditions.[4] For example, if a consumer orders a coffee cup from a website, receives a broken cup, and is not satisfied with the company's response to his inquiries, he may decide to post a negative review of the website online. If the company has written a non-disparagement clause into the terms and conditions of either the sales contract or the website itself, mandating that customers do nothing to damage the reputation or services of the company, it may elect to sue its customer for breach of contract due to his negative review, even if the review is accurate. Indeed, the consumer may not even be allowed to post a photo of the broken cup.

The owners of the website *KlearGear.com* were brought to Utah's Federal district court over a non-disparagement clause the website placed in its terms of sale "in an effort to ensure fair and honest public feedback."[5] A couple who never received their order and left a negative review on the website Ripoff Report was contacted several years later by KlearGear with a demand for $3,500 for violating the non-disparagement clause.[6] The Utah court found in favor of the reviewers, awarding over $300,000 in compensatory and punitive damages, but other consumers elsewhere may not be so fortunate. As a result of this highly publicized case, some states have begun enacting legislation to protect their citizens from non-negotiated non-disparagement clauses. For example, California recently passed a law prohibiting non-disparagement clauses in consumer goods or services contracts—unless they are knowingly and voluntarily negotiated.[7]

Non-Disparagement Clauses Undermine the Functioning of Digital Markets, Hurting Consumers and Businesses

One of the defining features of the digital economy is that customers can provide ratings of companies, products, and services—a phenomenon frequently referred to as the "wisdom of the crowd." Pioneering online services like Amazon, TripAdvisor, and Yelp, as well as many other websites, empower consumers to make more-informed decisions by presenting this crowd-sourced information alongside merchants' own descriptions of their products and services. This feedback is especially important when consumers are making purchases online, since they will not always have had the opportunity to evaluate products or sellers in person. Indeed, multiple empirical studies have found that customers rely on consumer reviews to make purchasing decisions and that better reviews lead to greater sales.[8] For example, one study found that a one-star increase in a restaurant's rating on Yelp led to a 5 percent to 9 percent increase in revenue.[9] Not surprisingly, many of the newest, rapidly growing Internet-based businesses, such as Uber, Airbnb, and Etsy, have integrated user-feedback as a key feature of their digital platforms.

A major purpose of reviews is to create an effective feedback loop: Consumers buy a product or service, and then review it online or elsewhere, so that other consumers can take those reviews into consideration before making purchases. Companies can change their products or services in response to compliments and complaints—and then, when they improve poorly reviewed features or add new ones, consumers can provide new reviews. Or other consumers, now empowered with more accurate information in the marketplace, can choose to buy from another company. Limiting these reviews to only positive feedback (*i.e.,* comments that would not damage the company's reputation), significantly reduces the benefit of these processes for consumers, because they lose access to accurate information and may make suboptimal purchasing decisions.

Companies gain important insights about how best to meet the needs of their customers by data mining customer reviews. These tools depend on accurate and complete information. For example, L.L. Bean purportedly investigates products that continually receive ratings of less than three stars. After a certain variety of fitted sheets received a large volume of negative online reviews, the company found a manufacturing defect, took the sheets off the market, and offered 6,300 new sets to customers who had purchased the faulty variety.[10]

If companies are not receiving negative feedback, then they are not using this feedback to improve their offerings, and consumers are receiving lower-quality goods and services.[11] Indeed, one recent study found that after hotels begin responding to online user reviews, regardless of whether the reviews are good, neutral, or negative, they begin to receive higher ratings from guests—presumably because hotel managers are incorporating customer feedback.[12] Another e-commerce solutions provider found that customers who saw a company response to a negative review were almost twice as likely to make a purchase as those who saw negative reviews without a company response; and overall opinion of the product became twice as positive.[13] Thus, the opportunity to share honest reviews can benefit companies and service providers by offering a quality-control platform, and it can benefit consumers by offering an opportunity to air grievances and have them addressed.

Accurate reviews improve the functioning of markets. Indeed, it has long been an axiom in economics that markets work best when both parties—the buyer and the seller—have more information. In particular, better information enables consumers to make better choices. Some of those choices may result in some companies or service providers going out of business or losing business as potential customers learn of the poor quality of their products and services and opt to buy elsewhere. But by definition, this means that the market share of more efficient or higher-quality sellers increases, thereby maximizing overall economic welfare.

Some companies may be concerned about how false reviews can unfairly hurt their businesses, and this is a legitimate concern as their employees' jobs and welfare also are at stake. Competing businesses may try to manipulate consumer opinion by posting fake reviews—either positive ones for their own products and services or negative ones for a rival's.[14] The answer to this problem is not to limit all negative reviews, but rather to minimize those that are false or misleading.

Online platforms recognize the importance of accurate reviews for their users, and so they have invested in technology to detect fraudulent reviews.[15] For example, Yelp automatically filters out reviews that it suspects are fraudulent, and the site even issues pop-up alerts to consumers who visit the profile page of a business that it has caught buying fake reviews.[16] Some state attorneys general have also fined businesses for posting fake reviews as this violated their truth-in-advertising laws.[17] While digital platforms have taken many steps to limit bias in online reviews, if some businesses are using anti-disparagement clauses to silence their critics, then online reviews for these industries will be misleading and consumers will be worse off.

Congress Should Protect Consumers' Right to Review

Using non-disparagement clauses to silence negative public feedback undermines a key part of the digital economy and makes many consumers and business worse off. Given the clear negative impact of biased reviews for both consumers and businesses, Congress should intervene to prohibit these clauses in consumer contracts. Specifically, Congress should pass the bipartisan Consumer Review Freedom Act of 2015, introduced by Sens. John Thune (R–SD), Brian Schatz (D–HI), and Jerry Moran (R–KS), which would take two important steps to address this problem. First, the legislation would void anti-disparagement clauses in consumer contracts if they restrict consumers from publicly reviewing products or businesses in good faith. Second, the legislation would authorize the Federal Trade Commission to take action against businesses that insert these provisions into their contracts for engaging in unfair and deceptive practices.

Moreover, this legislation would still allow companies to take action against individuals who post false and defamatory reviews. In addition to bringing defamation cases against individuals who post patently false statements about their products and services, companies also can work with platforms to remove false statements. Virtually every online platform includes terms of service prohibiting unlawful statements and provides a mechanism to help business owners have untruthful statements removed. For example, business owners can flag potentially fake reviews on Yelp with a single click.[18]

Notably, this legislation takes a narrow approach to address a very specific consumer harm. The legislation would not apply to non-disparagement clauses found in voluntarily negotiated agreements, such as employment agreements or divorce settlements, where parties may have a legitimate interest in agreeing to certain terms.

Conclusion

Protecting people's speech is important first and foremost as a First Amendment issue. Protections, such as those offered in the Consumer Review Freedom Act, would help ensure that individuals have the right to engage in lawful forms of speech and that others can benefit from the information conveyed in this protected speech. In addition, protecting online speech, especially complaints or criticisms, is necessary to ensure that online markets function efficiently by giving consumers access to unbiased feedback about the products and services they research. While states have made some progress in laying the foundation for legislation prohibiting non-disparagement clauses, the U.S. Congress should step in to create a baseline of protection for all citizens' basic rights to freedom of expression in the digital marketplace.

References

[1] Lucille M. Ponte, "Protecting Band Image or Gaming the System? Consumer 'Gag' Contracts in an Age of Crowdsourced Ratings and Review," *William & Mary Business Law Review* (forthcoming), March 16, 2015, http://papers.ssrn.com/sol3/papers.cfm?abstract\id=2579172.

[2] *Ibid.*

[3] Chris Morran, "Wedding Company Contract Tries To Ban Bride & Groom From 'Encouraging' Negative Feedback," *Consumerist*, April 20, 2015, http://consumerist.com/2015/04/20/wedding-company-contract-tries-to-ban-bride-groom-from-encouraging-negative-feedback/.

[4] Noah Davis, "The Yelper and the Negative Review: the Developing Battle Over Nondisparagement Clauses," *American Bar Association*, Vol. 3, No. 10, May 2014, http://www.americanbar.org/publications/gpsolo\report/2014/may\2014/yelper\negative\review\developing\battle\nondisparagement\clauses.html.

[5] Chris Morran, "KlearGear.com Ordered To Pay $306K To Couple Who Wrote Negative Review," *Consumerist*, June 26, 2014, http://consumerist.com/2014/06/26/kleargear-com-ordered-to-pay-306k-to-couple-who-wrote-negative-review/.

[6] *Ibid.*

[7] California Assembly Bill No. 2365, Unlawful contracts, §1670.8 (2014), http://leginfo.legislature.ca.gov/faces/billNavClient.xhtml?bill\id=201320140AB2365.

[8] Judith Chevalier and Dina Mayzil, "The Effect of Word of Mouth on Sales: Online Book Reviews," *Journal of Marketing Research* (August 2006), 345–354, https://msbfile03.usc.edu/digitalmeasures/mayzlin/intellcont/chevalier\mayzlin06-1.pdf.

[9] Michael Luca, "Reviews, Reputation, and Revenue: The Case of Yelp.com," *Harvard Business School* (2011), http://www.hbs.edu/faculty/Publication%20Files/12-016\0464f20e-35b2-492e-a328-fb14a325f718.pdf.

[10] Shelly Banjo, "Firms Take Online Reviews to Heart," *Wall Street Journal*, July 29, 2012, http://www.wsj.com/articles/SB10001424052702303292204577517394043189230.

[11] Erin Mulligan Nelson, "Why Terrible Online Reviews Are Actually Good For You," *Advertising Age*, September 15, 2011, http://adage.com/article/digitalnext/terrible-online-reviews-good/229790/; Shelly Banjo, "Firms Take Online Reviews to Heart."

[12] Davide Proserpio and Georgios Zervas, ''Online Reputational Management: Estimating the Impact of Management Responses on Consumer Reviews,'' *Boston University School of Management Research Paper* (2014), September 27, 2015, http://papers.ssrn.com/sol3/Papers.cfm?abstract_id=2521190.

[13] ''The Conversation Index,'' *Bazaar Voice*, Vol. 6, accessed April 2, 2015, 11, http://media2.bazaarvoice.com/documents/Bazaarvoice\Conversation\Index\Volume6.pdf.

[14] Dina Mayzlin, Yaniv Dover, and Judy Chevalier, ''Promotional Reviews: An Empirical Investigation of Online Review Manipulation,'' *American Economic Review* 104 (2014), 2421–55.

[15] Michael Luca and Georgios Zervas, ''Fake it Till You Make It: Reputation, Competition, and Yelp Review Fraud,'' *Harvard Business School*, May 1, 2015, http://papers.ssrn.com/sol3/papers.cfm?abstract_id=2293164.

[16] Eric Singley, ''Consumer alerts: because you might like to know . . .'' *Yelp Official Blog*, October 18, 2012, http://officialblog.yelp.com/2012/10/consumer-alerts-because-you-might-like-to-know.html.

[17] Julie Bort, ''New York Attorney General Busts 19 Companies For Writing Fake Yelp Reviews'', *Business Insider*, September 23, 2013, http://www.businessinsider.com/new-york-cracks-down-on-fake-yelp-reviews-2013-9.

[18] See Yelp, ''Terms of Service,'' October 13, 2015, http://www.yelp.com/static?country=US&p=tos.

The CHAIRMAN. Thank you, Mr. Atkinson.
Next up is Ms. Palmer. Please share your story.

STATEMENT OF JENNIFER KULAS PALMER, PLAINTIFF, PALMER V. KLEARGEAR

Ms. PALMER. Chairman Thune, Ranking Member Nelson, and members of the Committee, thank you for inviting me to testify today. My name is Jen Palmer, and my family's ordeal with a bullying company that tried to fine us for a negative review demonstrates why non-disparagement clauses should be prohibited.

In December 2008, my husband, John Palmer, placed an order from the online merchant KlearGear for a couple of small desk trinkets that came to less than $20. When the items failed to arrive, we both attempted to contact the company through phone and e-mail. Though we never got a human being on the phone, the e-mail responses claimed that the order was never paid for and was thus canceled.

Frustrated at the shoddy customer service, I posted a review of KlearGear on *RipoffReport.com*, and we moved on with our lives.

Then, in May 2012, John got an e-mail from KlearGear demanding that my review be removed within 72 hours or we would be fined $3,500 for violating the non-disparagement clause in their terms of sale and use.

This clause, which barred customers from, ''taking any action that negatively impacts *KlearGear.com*, its reputation, products, services, management, or employees,'' didn't exist when John ordered the items, and the fact that John didn't write the review didn't matter to them. Researching via the Internet archives confirmed that the clause didn't appear until February 2012, 3 years after my review had been posted.

We were shocked and scared. I spent hours researching how to remove the review, only to find that *RipoffReport.com* has a policy of not removing reviews. John tried explaining to KlearGear that the review could not be removed, that the non-disparagement clause didn't exist at the time he tried to place the order, and that he didn't write the review, I did.

KlearGear responded by threatening to report the $3,500 fine as a debt to the credit bureaus. This frightened us so much that we purchased a credit-monitoring service for John. Three months later, the negative report for $3,500, with KlearGear as the creditor, appeared on his credit report.

We immediately disputed the debt with the credit bureaus, with no success. KlearGear again e-mailed us and repeated their position, admitting they had confirmed the debt as valid. But we couldn't afford to hire an attorney and didn't know how to fix our credit report without legal help. It would be more than 18 months before John's credit would be clean again.

We have been very careful to live within our means, using financing only for large purchases like our cars in 2008 and 2011, our house in 2009, and medical bills that weren't covered by insurance. We had no problems getting financing for any of those. But for a year and a half, KlearGear's black mark on John's credit caused us constant anxiety, fear, and humiliation when people would ask us, "Who is KlearGear, and why do you owe them $3,500?"

Because of the credit problems, we were denied a credit card, delayed on a car loan, and deterred from trying to buy a new home that would move us closer to our workplaces. The worst came when we were denied emergency financing to replace a broken furnace in October 2013.

We were desperate, wrapping our then-3-year-old son Damien in blankets every night as temperatures dropped near freezing. I was terrified, too scared to tell anyone for fear that social services would take Damien away from us because we had no heat. We had to cut every expense that month, and, between both our paychecks that month, we were able to buy a basic furnace with cash.

By that point, we were tired of living in constant anxiety and fear. I contacted a reporter at KUTV in Salt Lake City, who did a segment on our plight and got us in contact with the nonprofit organization Public Citizen, which represented us in suing KlearGear.

They helped us to clear up John's credit, and we won a default judgment against KlearGear. After bullying us for so long, KlearGear never even bothered to show up to defend themselves in court.

Throughout our entire ordeal, we only wanted two things: that all traces of KlearGear's actions against us be cleared from John's credit and to do everything we could to ensure nobody else ever had to experience the nightmare we endured.

We want Congress to ban non-disparagement clauses, and we applaud the Committee for proposing to address the problem by giving the Federal Trade Commission and State authorities the power to go after unscrupulous companies that use them.

We aren't the only victims of this type of conduct, as Public Citizen has reported several times on their website and blog. Companies should not have the power to restrict consumer speech or punish people who criticize them. It needs to stop. Companies should earn their reputations honestly with good products and services and fair dealing.

We think states should be free to enforce this law in every way they can. I was glad to hear that a restriction barring States' Attorneys General's offices from hiring outside attorneys is being removed.

I am grateful for the opportunity to share my experience with you. On behalf of my husband, John, my son, Damien, and all the consumers out there who are being bullied and silenced by companies wielding non-disparagement clauses, I urge you to pass a bill that prohibits these clauses and provides for robust enforcement of the law.

Thank you.

[The prepared statement of Ms. Palmer follows:]

PREPARED STATEMENT OF JENNIFER KULAS PALMER, PLAINTIFF, PALMER V. KLEAR

Thank you for inviting me to testify today. My name is Jen Palmer, and I live with my husband and son in Hillsboro, Oregon. I'm here to tell you about my experiences with a non-disparagement clause and the company that tried to make my family pay $3,500 because I wrote a critical review online, and how they ruined my husband's credit when we refused to pay. My story shows what can happen when companies are allowed to use non-disparagement clauses in their contracts to bully consumers. And it shows why Congress should take action to prohibit the use of these clauses in consumer contracts.

Just before Christmas 2008, when we lived in Utah, my husband John Palmer placed an order from an online merchant called KlearGear. He ordered a desk toy and a keychain as Christmas gifts, and he paid for them when he ordered. The whole order cost less than $20 including shipping.

The items never arrived. John and I both tried to call the company, but calling the numbers on the company's website only got us automated responses, never a human being. We tried e-mailing, and the customer service person claimed that the order was never paid for and they had ultimately cancelled the order.

We were incredibly frustrated by the shoddy service and the impossibility of reaching anyone. In Feburary 2009, I posted a review expressing my opinions on the site *RipoffReport.com*. We went on with our lives and considered it a lesson learned never to deal with them again.

More than three years later, in May 2012, out of the blue, John received an e-mail from KlearGear demanding that John have the review on *RipoffReport.com* removed within 72 hours, or pay KlearGear $3,500 for violations of their Terms of Sale and Use. We were shocked and scared by the demand. It seemed this could not be legal. KlearGear claimed that my review violated a "non-disparagement clause" in KlearGear's Terms of Sale and Use, the text of which barred the customer—who was John, not me, but that didn't matter to them—from "taking any action that negatively impacts *KlearGear.com*, its reputation, products, services, management or employees." John did some research via the Internet Archive and was able to discover that the clause wasn't even present in the Terms of Sale when he placed his order back in December 2008. He found that the clause did not appear until February 2012.

I spent hours researching how to remove the report from *RipoffReport.com*, because we were scared and didn't know what else to do. But RipoffReport has a policy of not removing reviews, so we were stuck. John tried explaining to KlearGear that the "non-disparagement clause" was not in the Terms of Sale and Use at the time of John's order from KlearGear; that it was I, not John, who wrote the review; and *RipoffReport.com*'s policy of not removing reviews meant we had no control over whether the review remained online. The person claiming to be KlearGear's legal representative just reiterated to us that "this matter will remain open until the published content is removed," and threatened to report the $3500 as a debt to the credit reporting agencies. We didn't think they could do something so outrageous, but those e-mails had disturbed us enough that we purchased a credit monitoring service for John's credit.

About three months later, our fears were realized. In August 2012, a negative report appeared on John's credit reports from two of the three major credit reporting agencies, reflecting a $3,500 debt with KlearGear as creditor. We immediately called Experian and Equifax to dispute the debt. Then KlearGear e-mailed John again and said we owed yet another $50 under its "Chargeback/Dispute Policy," which said that we had to give KlearGear 30 days to resolve any billing dispute before going to a third party. We tried to tell KlearGear they couldn't charge us any of this money, but they just repeated their position and even admitted that they confirmed to Experian that the debt was valid. I spent hours on the phone with the credit bureaus, contacting local law firms to help us, and even doing some legal research myself. Despite all the information I found, we couldn't afford to hire an attorney and we didn't know how to fix the credit report without legal help.

It took more than 18 months to remove the blemish from John's credit, and not until after the non-profit organization Public Citizen filed a lawsuit on our behalf. In the meantime, that bad credit report caused us all kinds of problems. We have been very careful to live within our means, using financing only for large purchases like the house, cars, and medical bills that weren't covered by insurance. We'd had no trouble getting loans to buy a car in 2008, our house in 2009, or another car in 2011.

But now for the times we needed credit, we couldn't get it. For instance, we were held up for a month on a car loan in late 2012. Even worse than the delay was the humiliation of having to explain everything and the anxiety of whether or not this was going to go through, especially because at that point, we really needed a second car. I specifically remember the Finance Manager at the dealership saying to us "Who is KlearGear and why do you owe them $3,500?" John was also denied a credit card around the same time, and we began to fear we'd never get a loan for anything again.

We were also hoping to sell our house and buy another one in the winter of 2013, because both of us were commuting more than 30 miles each, which was a particular hardship since our son, Damien, was just 3. We were scared to even try to get the credit we'd need to make necessary repairs on our home and to buy a new one. We didn't want to go through that humiliation again. Having the initial denials on the car froze us in our financial tracks and gave us a serious case of "once bitten, 17 times shy."

The worst consequence of KlearGear's retaliation against us occurred in October 2013, more than a year after KlearGear reported the supposed "debt." In July and September we had needed two major plumbing repairs on our home which had depleted our savings, and then our furnace broke at the beginning of October. We couldn't afford to buy a new one with cash and the weather was turning cold. I contacted several companies for financing, but no one could approve us. At that point we were desperate, wrapping Damien in blankets every night, when the weather was regularly dropping to around freezing. I was terrified—I had no idea how long this would go on. I was scared social services would come and take Damien, saying we were bad parents because we couldn't even keep the heat on. We cut as many expenses as we could that month. I dreaded each weather forecast. Between both our paychecks, after a few weeks we had saved enough money to buy the most basic furnace with cash.

By that point, we were tired of living in fear and not being able to get emergency credit for basic needs. We spoke to a reporter at KUTV in Salt Lake City who did a segment on our plight, and eventually got us in contact with Public Citizen, which represented us in suing KlearGear. Public Citizen helped us clear up John's credit, finally, and we won a default judgment against KlearGear, who after bullying us for years never even bothered to show up to defend itself in court.

Now that part of our lives is behind us. We were able to sell the house and move to Oregon for a work opportunity. Damien is a healthy and happy 5 year old.

Throughout our entire ordeal, we only wanted two things: that all traces of KlearGear's actions against us be cleared from John's credit, and to do everything we could to ensure nobody else ever had to experience the nightmare we endured.

We want Congress to ban non-disparagement clauses, which lead to the silencing of ordinary people and to bullying tactics like those KlearGear used to make us feel anxious, terrified, humiliated and helpless for more than a year. And we aren't the only victims of this type of conduct. If you read Public Citizen's website and its blog, you'll see that a Wisconsin woman was threatened with round-the-clock harassment by debt collectors for just telling an online retailer that she wanted to call her credit card company, a New Jersey woman was told she'd have to pay thousands of dollars in legal fees just to be able to post a critical online review of a website, and a New York hotel threatened couples holding weddings there that they'd be fined for negative reviews by their guests. The bullying and silencing of consumers needs to stop.

We applaud the Committee for proposing to address the problem of non-disparagement clauses. We like the idea of giving the Federal Trade Commission and state authorities the power to go after unscrupulous companies that use non-disparagement clauses. Companies should not have the power to restrict consumer speech or punish people who criticize them. Companies should have to earn their reputations honestly with good products and services, and fair dealing.

But we also believe that the bill as currently proposed must be strengthened. Specifically, one section prohibits state attorney general's offices from hiring outside attorneys to help enforce the prohibition on non-disparagement clauses. We don't think there ought to be restrictions on state enforcement powers, particularly because some smaller states might not have the resources to enforce every law with their own attorneys. We think states should be free to enforce this law however they can. There's no reason to limit the ways states can enforce it, particularly when states can hire outside lawyers for other purposes. Therefore I have been pleased to learn that the Committee intends to amend the bill to eliminate this restriction.

I'm grateful for the opportunity to share my experience with you. On behalf of my husband John, my son Damien, and all the consumers out there who are being bullied and silenced by companies wielding non-disparagement clauses, I urge you to pass a bill that both prohibits these clauses and provides for robust enforcement of the law.

Thank you.

The CHAIRMAN. Thank you, Ms. Palmer, for your willingness to share that story and be with us today.

Professor Goldman?

STATEMENT OF ERIC GOLDMAN, PROFESSOR, SANTA CLARA UNIVERSITY SCHOOL OF LAW

Mr. GOLDMAN. Mr. Chairman Thune, Ranking Member Nelson, and members of the Committee, I appreciate the opportunity to discuss the Consumer Review Freedom Act of 2015 and how Congress can help protect consumer reviews. I commend the Committee and the bill's sponsors for their leadership on this topic.

Consumer reviews are vitally important to our modern economy. Markets become stronger and more efficient when consumers share their marketplace experiences and guide other consumers toward the best vendors and away from poor ones.

Despite the social benefits generated by consumer reviews, some businesses try to distort their public reputation by contractually suppressing reviews from their customers. These efforts are categorically illegitimate. The Consumer Review Freedom Act will ensure every consumer has the opportunity to add their voice to the discourse so that other consumers can benefit from their experiences.

Because contractual restrictions on consumer reviews are such a terrible idea, it seems like existing law should already prohibit such practices. Although there are some precedents to support that position, I will explore two reasons why I think we still need the Consumer Review Freedom Act.

First, it is not clear if courts will enforce anti-review clauses. And I use the term "anti-review clauses" to describe what other people are calling gag contracts or clauses or non-disparagement clauses. We do have a nomenclature problem, and I am sorry for compounding that.

Many judges will refuse to enforce anti-review clauses for unconscionability, public policy, or other reasons, but judges also don't like to override contractual provisions, and so anti-review clauses are not guaranteed to fail in court.

I would like to call your attention, in particular, to a case, *Galland* v. *Johnston,* which involved a vacation rental contract that required tenants to agree that they would not, quote, "use blogs or websites for complaints, anonymously or not."

We don't have any idea how many consumers were deterred by this clause from sharing their experiences, but we do know that two tenants did post public reviews of the vacation rental online in defiance of the ban. The landlord then sued these tenants in Federal court.

The court held that the reviews weren't defamatory but the tenants, nevertheless, may have breached the rental contract. In other words, this ruling means that anti-review clauses expose the tenants to potential liability for sharing what was a non-defamatory review.

The Consumer Review Freedom Act will eliminate any ambiguity over the enforceability of anti-review clauses. It will mean that vacation tenants and all other customers will enjoy legal certainty about their rights to speak up.

The second reason why we need the Consumer Review Freedom Act is that businesses are always seeking ways to shape and manage their online reputations. As they offer the illusion of control, anti-review clauses will keep proliferating unless they are banned.

The experience of the healthcare industry illustrates how that might happen. In the late 2000s, a company called Medical Justice sold form contracts to doctors and other health-care professionals that contained anti-review clauses. Medical Justice's sales pitch to the doctors and healthcare professionals was elegant and tempting. It implied that, by using its form contracts, doctors and healthcare professionals would seemingly obtain a magic wand to scrub unwanted patient reviews from the Internet.

Over the years, I estimate that over a thousand doctors and other healthcare professionals deployed such anti-review clauses and that over a million Americans signed such provisions.

The long-term marketplace damages attributable to Medical Justice's misguided campaign is incalculable. Although Medical Justice changed its position in 2011 and told consumers to stop using its form, even today in 2015 it can be hard to find robust numbers of patient reviews for many healthcare providers.

Although the healthcare industry's adoption of anti-review contracts may seem to be an extreme case, we are likely to see similar effects in other industries dominated by small businesses and professional service providers. Why these categories of businesses? In many cases, these proprietors' self-identities are closely linked to their professional reputations. Negative feedback about their business feels like it reflects upon them as an individual.

If a vacation tenant says she didn't like the rental's decor, the landlord might take that as a criticism of her aesthetic tastes. Or if a patient says she didn't like her doctor's bedside manner, the doctor may feel like her personality is being criticized. Small-business owners and professional service providers will be attracted to anti-review clauses to prevent these public ego blows.

Therefore, without the Consumer Review Freedom Act, I expect other industries will embrace anti-review clauses like the healthcare industry did, and we as consumers will all be poorer for it.

Consumer reviews are worth fighting for, and I am thrilled to see Congress taking on that fight. I want to thank you for your work on the bill and for the opportunity to share my views.

[The prepared statement of Mr. Goldman follows:]

PREPARED STATEMENT OF ERIC GOLDMAN, PROFESSOR, SANTA CLARA UNIVERSITY SCHOOL OF LAW

Members of the Committee:

I appreciate this opportunity to discuss the Consumer Review Freedom Act of 2015 and how Congress can help protect consumer reviews. I commend the Committee, and the bill sponsors, for their leadership on this topic.

Consumer reviews are vitally important to our modern economy. Markets become stronger and more efficient when consumers share their marketplace experiences and guide other consumers toward the best vendors and away from poor ones.

Despite the social benefits generated by consumer reviews, some businesses try to distort their public reputation by contractually suppressing reviews from their customers. These efforts are categorically illegitimate. The Consumer Review Freedom Act will ensure every consumer has the opportunity to add their voice to the discourse so that other consumers can benefit from their experiences.

Because contractual restrictions on consumer reviews are such a terrible idea, it seems like existing law should already prohibit such practices. Although there is some precedent to support that conclusion, I'll explore two reasons why we still need the Consumer Review Freedom Act.

First, it's not clear if courts will enforce anti-review clauses.[1] Many judges will refuse to do so for unconscionability, public policy or other reasons. However, judges don't like to override contracts, so anti-review contracts aren't guaranteed to fail in court.

For example, in *Galland* v. *Johnston*,[2] a vacation rental contract required tenants to agree that they would not "use blogs or websites for complaints, anonymously or not." We have no idea how many tenants self-censored due to this contract clause, but we know two tenants defied the ban and criticized the vacation rental online. The landlord sued the tenants in Federal court. The court held that the reviews weren't defamatory but the tenants nevertheless may have breached the rental contract. This ruling means the anti-review clause exposed the tenants to liability for sharing non-defamatory reviews.

The Consumer Review Freedom Act will eliminate any ambiguity over the enforceability of anti-review clauses. It will mean that vacation tenants—and all other customers—will enjoy legal certainty about their rights to speak up.

The second reason we need the Consumer Review Freedom Act is that businesses are always seeking ways to shape and manage their online reputations. As they offer the illusion of such control, anti-review clauses will keep proliferating unless they are banned.

The experiences of the healthcare industry illustrate how this might happen. In the late 2000s, a company called Medical Justice sold form contracts to doctors and other healthcare professionals that contained anti-review clauses.[3] Medical Justice's sale pitch was elegant and tempting: by using its form contract, doctors and healthcare professionals would seemingly get a magic wand to scrub unwanted patient reviews from the Internet. Over the years, I estimate that over 1,000 healthcare professionals adopted Medical Justice's form contract and over 1 million Americans signed an anti-review contract.

The long-term marketplace damage attributable to Medical Justice's misguided campaign is incalculable. Although Medical Justice changed its position in 2011 and told its customers to stop using its forms, even today in 2015 it can be hard to find robust numbers of patient reviews for many healthcare providers.

Although the healthcare industry's adoption of anti-review contracts may be an extreme case, we're likely to see similar effects in other industries dominated by small businesses and professional service providers.

Why small businesses and professional service providers? In many cases, these proprietors' self-identities are closely linked to their professional reputations. Negative feedback about their business feels like it reflects on them as an individual. If a vacation tenant says she didn't like the rental's décor, the landlord might take that as criticism of her aesthetic tastes. Or if a patient says that she didn't like her doctor's bedside manner, the doctor may feel like her personality is being criticized.

---

[1] Unfortunately, there is no widely accepted term to describe the types of contract clauses at issue here. I use the term "anti-review clauses," but the terms "gag clauses" and "non-disparagement clauses" are also used. I don't prefer the latter because businesses sometimes attempt to restrict all reviews, positive and negative.

[2] Galland v. Johnston, 2015 WL 1290775 (S.D.N.Y. Mar. 19, 2015), http://law.justia.com/cases/federal/district-courts/new-york/nysdce/1:2014cv04411/428591/32/.

[3] The exact terms of the anti-review clause varied over the years. At some points, the contract banned reviews; other times, the contract assigned the IP rights to the patients' reviews.

Small business owners and professional service providers will be attracted to anti-review clauses to prevent these public ego blows. Therefore, without the Consumer Review Freedom Act, I expect other industries will embrace anti-review clauses like the healthcare industry did—and we as consumers will be poorer for those efforts.

Consumer reviews are worth fighting for, and I'm thrilled to see Congress taking on that fight. I thank you for your work on the bill and for the opportunity to share my views.

Attachments

- Eric Goldman, *How Congress Can Protect Online Consumer Reviews*, Forbes Tertium Quid, Nov. 2, 2015, *http://www.forbes.com/sites/ericgoldman/2015/11/02/how-congress-can-protect-online-consumer-reviews/*.
- Eric Goldman, *Court Might Enforce A Contract Ban On Consumer Reviews*, Forbes Tertium Quid, Mar. 27, 2015, *http://www.forbes.com/sites/ericgoldman/2015/03/27/court-might-enforce-a-contract-ban-on-consumer-reviews/*.
- Eric Goldman, *California Tells Businesses: Stop Trying To Ban Consumer Reviews*, Forbes Tertium Quid, Sept. 10, 2014, *http://www.forbes.com/sites/ericgoldman/2014/09/10/california-tells-businesses-stop-trying-to-ban-consumer-reviews/*.
- Eric Goldman, *Fining Customers For Negative Online Reviews Isn't New . . . Or Smart*, Forbes Tertium Quid, Aug. 7, 2014, *http://www.forbes.com/sites/ericgoldman/2014/08/07/fining-customers-for-negative-online-reviews-isnt-new-or-smart/*.
- Eric Goldman, *The Regulation of Reputational Information* in THE NEXT DIGITAL DECADE: ESSAYS ON THE FUTURE OF THE INTERNET 193 (Berin Szoka & Adam Marcus eds.) (2010), *http://ssrn.com/abstract=1754628*.
- Eric Goldman, *Patients' Online Reviews of Physicians*, MEDICAL ETHICS (a journal published by Lahey Health), Fall 2013, at 6, *http://ssrn.com/abstract=2367092*.

HOW CONGRESS CAN PROTECT ONLINE CONSUMER REVIEWS

Nov 2, 2015 @ 11:52 AM

For many Americans, the First Amendment is the alpha and omega of free speech protection. However, the First Amendment just sets a minimum level of free speech in our society. Legislatures, including Congress, may freely enact laws that go beyond the First Amendment to protect free speech. If done properly, those laws can help free speech more than the First Amendment.

The Consumer Review Freedom Act of 2015 (S. 2044 and H.R. 2110) is an example of a law that would helpfully supplement the First Amendment's protection of free speech. The Act would prevent businesses from contractually restricting their customers from reviewing them online (what I call "anti-review clauses"). Although it may be hard to believe any business would ever ask its customers to do something so anti-consumer, it's likely that millions of Americans have agreed to such clauses. The Consumer Review Freedom Act would benefit them–and all of us.

About The Act

(Note: I'll critique and quote the Senate bill's language, but the House and Senate versions are pretty similar).

The Act defines "covered communications" to include written, verbal or photographic consumer reviews. The Act says that any form contracts that ban, impose fines for, or attempt to obtain the intellectual property rights to, covered communications are void. The Act also declares such contracts unlawful and authorizes the Federal government and state attorneys' general to bring enforcement actions for imposing such contracts (the House bill designates the U.S. Department of Justice as the principal Federal enforcement entity; the Senate bill, the Federal Trade Commission).

What's Good

Some of the best aspects of the Act:

- Broad Definition. Consumers can critique businesses in lots of ways. The Act's multi-media definition of "covered communications" should be broad enough to cover all of those possibilities.
- Broad Prohibitions. Businesses seeking to gag their consumers have tried many different contract tricks. The Act prohibits all of the known tricks (bans, fines

and IP assignments), so it will not be easy for a business to skirt around this law.

Recommended by Forbes

- Remedies. The Act makes anti-review clauses both void and unlawful. Void means that no court will enforce them, and unlawful means that it's illegal for businesses to include an anti-review clause in its form, even if the business never plans to enforce it.

Possible Tweaks

While I support the Act in its current form, a few tweaks are worth considering:

- Restriction to Form Contracts. The Act applies only when the anti-review clause is in a "form contract," defined as "a standardized contract used by a person and imposed on an individual without a meaningful opportunity for such individual to negotiate the standardized terms." This definition excludes individually negotiated non-disparagement clauses, which are sometimes found in settlement agreements. (A non-disparagement clause says that a person won't publicly say negative things–even if true–about someone else). Still, the statutory language leaves room for debate over whether a contract qualifies as a "form contract." Because I am skeptical that non-disparagement clauses are legitimate in any situation, I would favor extending the restrictions to all contracts, form or negotiated.
- Trade Secret Exception. The Act does not apply to "trade secret" protections, which makes sense because businesses should have the ability to protect their trade secrets. Unfortunately, businesses sometimes have ridiculously overexpansive views about what constitutes their trade secrets–including asserting that information disclosures to customers in ordinary buying-and-selling interactions constitute the business' trade secrets. To preserve trade secret protection but curb abusive overreaching, the Act could specify that ordinary business-consumer interactions can't qualify as trade secret disclosures.
- No Consumer Redress. The Act doesn't give consumers any affirmative recourse if a business attempts to impose or enforce an anti-review clause. This could be fixed in two ways. First, if a business makes the unwise decision to bring a lawsuit based on an anti-review clause, the court should award attorneys' fees and other defense costs to the consumer. Second, the statute should impose statutory damages on any businesses that includes anti-review clauses in their contracts.
- State Law Preemption. The Act doesn't preempt state laws (the Act says "Nothing in this section shall be construed to affect any cause of action brought by a person that exists or may exist under State law"). This might be a good thing because it increases the range of legal tools to combat anti-review clauses. On the other hand, one of the principal benefits of Federal law is that it can establish uniform rules across the country. Although I favor a multi-fronted effort to extinguish anti-review clauses, I probably favor legal uniformity a little more.

Aren't Anti-Review Clauses Already Illegal?

Because anti-review clauses are such an obviously terrible idea, such clauses are already running into legal trouble. For example, a 2003 New York case struck down an anti-review clause; the Department of Health and Human Service's Office for Civil Rights has told doctors they can't use anti-review clauses; in 2014, California enacted a law against businesses banning consumer reviews; and last month, the Federal Trade Commission obtained a preliminary injunction prohibiting Roca Labs from using anti-review clauses. With all of this precedent indicating that anti-review clauses aren't permissible, do we need a Federal law too?

Yes, we do. Anti-review clauses keep proliferating through different industries, so not every business has gotten the message. California's law is a helpful start, but that still leaves 49 states without comparable statutes. Plus, at least one case suggested that anti-review clauses may be enforceable. We need to put a decisive and unambiguous end t these anti-consumer, anti-competitive practices, and the Consumer Review Freedom Act would do just that.

A Final Thought

In addition to the Consumer Review Freedom Act, Congress should enact a Federal anti-SLAPP law–another example of how Congress can extend the First Amendment's free speech protections. Anti-SLAPP laws help protect consumers from businesses making spurious legal claims that negative consumer reviews are defamatory. Businesses often intimidate consumers into removing reviews by threatening costly legal action (even if the review is completely legitimate), so the procedural and financial protections in a Federal anti-SLAPP law would curb such abusive threats. The combination of the Consumer Review Freedom Act and Federal anti-SLAPP protection would provide a solid legal foundation for the continued growth and success of online consumer reviews.

forbes.com—http://www.forbes.com/sites/ericgoldman/2015/11/02/how-congress-can-protect-online-consumer-reviews/

COURT MIGHT ENFORCE A CONTRACT BAN ON CONSUMER REVIEWS

Mar 27, 2015 @ 11:04 AM

Claude and Violaine Galland own an apartment in Paris, France. They offer it for rental through VRBO, an online service for vacation rentals. The Gallands' rental agreement include the following language: "The tenants agree not to use blogs or websites for complaints, anonymously or not." Though clumsily worded, this clause is similar to prior attempts to restrict consumer reviews, such as the provisions used by doctors and dentists, hotels, apartment owners and other vacation rental services. As far as I know, no court has ever enforced any of these clauses purporting to suppress consumer reviews.

Two different renters, the Johnstons and Bowdens, rented the Gallands' apartment and subsequently posted critical reviews on VRBO. Mr. Galland allegedly offered $300–unsuccessfully–to the Bowdens to remove their post. Instead, the Gallands sued the Johnstons and Bowdens for defamation, breach of contract and other claims.

The judge dismissed the defamation claims–but refused to dismiss the breach of contract claim because:

> It is plausible that Defendants made the posts in violation of the contract. Moreover, it is plausible that such negative reviews could cause injuries to the Gallands' business. Nevertheless, these are questions for a trier of fact to decide. . .

Thus, the breach of contract claim will go to a trial to decide if the reviews violated the contract.

Surprisingly, the judge didn't discuss the illegality of the contract clause. In 2003, a New York court instructed a software vendor to stop banning consumer reviews in its contract (the exact restriction: "The customer will not publish reviews of this product without prior consent from Network Associates, Inc."). The court held that using such a clause may be a deceptive practice under New York's consumer protection law. I can't see any reason why the Gallands' clause wouldn't violate the same law. (The Gallands' case is being litigated in a New York Federal court applying New York law). Irrespective of the New York law, the contract restriction should be void as a matter of public policy. I'm hoping the court will come to its senses and realize that no trial is needed because the clause should be condemned, not enforced.

It's remarkable that anyone had the confidence to litigate such a clause at all. We have seen relatively few courtroom battles over contractual bans on consumer reviews, and we aren't likely to see many such disputes in the future. The Gallands' contract provision clearly violates California's new law against consumer review bans, and I believe a new Federal bill will be introduced to make such bans nationwide. Eventually vendors will get the message and stop trying. Until they do, we need more tools to discourage such clauses in the future–and to discourage wasteful litigation intended to suppress renters' rights to express themselves.

For more on this topic, see my article, The Regulation of Reputational Information.

Case citation: Galland v. Johnston, 2015 WL 1290775 (SDNY March 19, 2015)

forbes.com—http://www.forbes.com/sites/ericgoldman/2015/03/27/court-might-enforce-a-contract-ban-on-consumer-reviews/

CALIFORNIA TELLS BUSINESSES: STOP TRYING TO BAN CONSUMER REVIEWS

Sep 10, 2014 @ 12:46 PM

Increasingly, businesses are looking for ways to suppress or erase consumers' negative online reviews of them. In particular, we've recently seen a proliferation of contract clauses purporting to stop consumers from reviewing businesses online.

Those overreaching contract clauses have never been a good idea, but yesterday, the idea got worse. Gov. Jerry Brown signed AB 2365 into law, to be codified as California Civil Code Sec. 1670.8. The law is a first-in-the-nation statute to stop businesses from contractually gagging their consumers.

The new law says that a consumer contract "may not include a provision waiving the consumer's right to make any statement regarding the seller or lessor or its employees or agents, or concerning the goods or services." Any contract terms violating this provision are void. Simply including a prohibited clause in a contract, even if the business never enforces it, or threatening to enforce such a clause can lead to a penalty of up to $2,500 (up to $10,000 if the violation is willful). The penalties may be financially modest, but any California business foolish enough to take an anti-review contract to court will end up writing a check to their customers.

Instead of telling consumers they can't review the businesses, some businesses are imposing financial penalties on consumers for writing negative reviews. I recently wrote about a New York hotel's contract that fined customers $500 if they, or their wedding guests, posted negative online reviews. Disputes over fines will rarely end up in court because the hotel simply deducted the fine from the customer's security deposit. Or other businesses, such as KlearGear, have filed negative credit reports against consumers who didn't pay the fine. A consumer could challenge the security deposit deduction or negative credit report in court, but few will.

The statute tries to address the fining tactic by saying it's unlawful to "penalize a consumer for making any statement protected under this section." The statute doesn't define what statements are "protected under this section," so I'm not sure how courts will interpret the provision. The legislative history expressly references the KlearGear situation, so I anticipate the statute will cover fines against customers for writing negative online reviews.

We've also seen businesses use intellectual property claims to inhibit or discourage consumer reviews. The most notorious was the scheme by Medical Justice that helped doctors get their patients to assign the copyright in unwritten reviews. Unfortunately, the statute doesn't directly address this situation, and arguably these IP-based tactics don't constitute "waivers" prohibited by the statute. Perhaps courts will nevertheless interpret the statute to ban these abusive practices; otherwise, I fear we'll see more IP-based anti-review shenanigans following this law.

If you're responsible for your business' contract with consumers, today's a good day to review the contract and confirm that you don't have any language that might be interpreted as a restriction on your customers' ability to review your business. There are so many better ways to handle consumer reviews.

forbes.com—http://www.forbes.com/sites/ericgoldman/2014/09/10/california-tells-businesses-stop-trying-to-ban-consumer-reviews/

FINING CUSTOMERS FOR NEGATIVE ONLINE REVIEWS ISN'T NEW. . .OR SMART

Aug 7, 2014 @ 10:47 AM

This week, we learned that a New York hotel, the Union Street Guest House, was fining guests $500 for posting negative online reviews. The story received considerable media attention because the restriction violates our social norms and is almost certainly unlawful. Unfortunately, this is not the first time businesses have tried to control negative reviews online, a goal that some businesses apparently find irresistible. We shouldn't be surprised the next time we see businesses try to gag their customers, but it should make us mad. . .mad enough to demand new statutor punishments for businesses who disrespect their customers and the marketplace.

The Union Street Guest House Contract

Until recently, the Union Street Guest House included the following provision in its policies:

> If you stay here to attend a wedding and leave us a negative review on any Internet site you agree to a $500. fine for each negative review.
>
> If you have booked the Inn for a wedding or other type of event anywhere in the region and given us a deposit of any kind for guests to stay at USGH there will be a $500 fine that will be deducted from your deposit for every negative review of USGH placed on any Internet site by anyone in your party and/or attending your wedding or event (this is due to the fact that your guests may not understand what we offer and we expect you to explain that to them).

Allegedly, the guest house would refund the full deposit if the author removed the negative review.

We don't know how often the guest house actually fined its customers. Slate reported on one e-mail exchange where the policy was invoked. I imagine other guests simply removed negative reviews in response to threats by the guest house.

The guest house's provision stands out for two reasons. First, it purports to hold the bride or groom accountable for posts made by their wedding guests. However, newlyweds can't really control what their guests feel or say. Second, the guest house could self-implement the remedy by deducting money from the customer's deposit, rather than bringing a lawsuit in court–which would almost certainly fail.

Past Attempts To Suppress Negative Consumer Reviews

The Business Insider article said the guest house's provision was "a novel way to keep negative reviews off Yelp and other sites," but that's wrong. Although we've seen a range of ways businesses have tried to suppress online reviews, we've also seen this story before. Here's a short survey of some prior efforts to gag customers:

Late 1990s. Software vendor Network Associates obligated its end users to "not publish reviews of this product without prior consent from Network Associates, Inc." In 2003, a New York court enjoined Network Associates from using that clause.

2007–2011. A small company, Medical Justice, provided doctors and dentists with form contracts designed to veto any negative online reviews. The contracts initially banned online reviews outright. A division of the Federal Department of Health & Human Services held that it was unethical for doctors to suppress patients' reviews. Medical Justice eventually changed its form so that patients assigned the copyright in their unwritten online reviews of the doctor or dentist. Armed with the purported copyright, doctors and dentists could threaten review websites with copyright infringement for continuing to publish any reviews the doctor/dentist wanted gone (presumably, only negative reviews). I believe that over 1 million Americans signed some variation of Medical Justice's form contract. In 2011, Medical Justice "retired" its form and advised doctors and dentists to stop using it. Meanwhile, there remains a pending lawsuit by a patient against a dentist who tried to invoke the form to demand the removal of a negative review. That lawsuit is going poorly for the dentist. For more information on Medical Justice's anti-review efforts, see DoctoredReviews.com.

2012. We learned that some vacation rental companies were pulling the same basic stunt as the Union Street Guest House. Some contracts contained a clause restricting online reviews, styled as a non-disclosure agreement. For example, one provision said the customer may not "discuss or disclose the occupancy of the subject property with any entity not bound by the terms of this agreement without the expressed written authorization of the homeowner and the property agent representing the homeowner." Furthermore, the rental company retained the customer's security deposit and could deduct fines from there. I'm not aware of any legal tests of these contracts.

2013. Online retailer KlearGear attempted to restrict negative consumer reviews by imposing a fine, but the customer says that KlearGear's contract didn't actually contain the restriction at the time of purchase. When the customer failed to pay the fine, KlearGear reported the non-payment to the credit agencies, damaging the customer's credit. The customer is suing KlearGear for its behavior, and that lawsuit isn't going well for KlearGear.

In response to the KlearGear incident, a bill was introduced in California (AB2365) to ban surreptitious attempts to restrict customers' reviews. The bill has some obvious deficiencies, including the fact that the bill's language might no restrict the guest house's provision. Still, I think the bill is a sign of things to come. It hurts the marketplace when businesses keep customers from sharing their experiences with other prospective customers, so we simply cannot tolerate such efforts. If businesses can't resist their impulses to hide their failings, the legislatures will have to step in.

forbes.com—http://www.forbes.com/sites/ericgoldman/2014/08/07/fining-customers-for-negative-online-reviews-isnt-new-or-smart/

THE NEXT DIGITAL DECADE
ESSAYS ON THE FUTURE OF THE INTERNET

Edited by Berin Szoka & Adam Marcus

TECH FREEDOM

NextDigitalDecade.com

TechFreedom
techfreedom.org
Washington, D.C.

This work was published by TechFreedom (**TechFreedom.org**), a non-profit public policy think tank based in Washington, D.C. TechFreedom's mission is to unleash the progress of technology that improves the human condition and expands individual capacity to choose. We gratefully acknowledge the generous and unconditional support for this project provided by VeriSign, Inc.

More information about this book is available at **NextDigitalDecade.com**

ISBN 978-1-4357-6786-7

© 2010 by TechFreedom, Washington, D.C.

This work is licensed under the Creative Commons Attribution NonCommercial-ShareAlike 3.0 Unported License. To view a copy of this license, visit **http://creativecommons.org/licenses/by-nc-sa/3.0/** or send a letter to Creative Commons, 171 Second Street, Suite 300, San Francisco, California, 94105, USA.

Cover Designed by Jeff Fielding.

The Next Digital Decade: ESSAYS ON THE FUTURE OF THE INTERNET

THE REGULATION OF REPUTATIONAL INFORMATION

By Eric Goldman*

Introduction

This essay considers the role of reputational information in our marketplace. It explains how well-functioning marketplaces depend on the vibrant flow of accurate reputational information, and how misdirected regulation of reputational information could harm marketplace mechanisms. It then explores some challenges created by the existing regulation of reputational information and identifies some regulatory options for the future.

Reputational Information Defined

Typical definitions of "reputation" focus on third-party cognitive perceptions of a person.[1] For example, *Black's Law Dictionary* defines reputation as the "esteem in which a person is held by others."[2] Bryan Garner's *A Dictionary of Modern Legal Usage* defines reputation as "what one is thought by others to be."[3] The Federal Rules of Evidence also reflect this perception-centric view of "reputation."[4]

Although this definition is useful so far as it goes, I am more interested in how information affects prospective decision-making.[5] Accordingly, I define "reputational information" as follows:

> information about an actor's past performance that helps predict the actor's future ability to perform or to satisfy the decision-maker's preferences.

This definition contemplates that actors create a pool of data (both subjective and objective) through their conduct. This pool of data—the reputational information—can provide insights into the actor's likely future behavior.

Reputation Systems

"Reputation systems" aggregate and disseminate reputational information to consumers of that information. Reputation systems can be mediated or unmediated.

In unmediated reputation systems, the producers and consumers of reputational information communicate directly. Examples of unmediated reputation systems include word of mouth, letters of recommendation and job references.

In mediated reputation systems, a third-party publisher gathers, organizes and publishes reputational information. Examples of mediated reputation systems include the Better Business Bureau's ratings, credit reports/scores, investment ratings (such as Morningstar mutual fund ratings and Moody bond ratings), and consumer review sites.

The Internet has led to a proliferation of mediated reputation systems, and in particular consumer review sites.[6] Consumers can review just about anything online; examples include:

- eBay's feedback forum,[7] which allows eBay's buyers and sellers to rate each other.

---

*Associate Professor and Director, High Tech Law Institute, Santa Clara University School of Law. E-mail: *egoldman@gmail.com*. Website: *http://www.ericgoldman.org*. In addition to a stint as General Counsel of Epinions.com, a consumer review website now part of the eBay enterprise, I have provided legal or consulting advice to some of the other companies mentioned in this essay. I prepared this essay in connection with a talk at the Third Annual Conference on the Law and Economics of Innovation at George Mason University, May 2009.

[1] As one commentator explained:

Through one's actions, one relates to others and makes impressions on them. These impressions, taken as a whole, constitute an individual's reputation—that is, what other people think of you, to the extent that their thoughts arise from what they know about you, or think they know about you.

Elizabeth D. De Armond, *Frothy Chaos: Modern Data Warehousing and Old-Fashioned Defamation*, 41 VAL. U.L. REV. 1061, 1065 (2007).

[2] BLACK'S LAW DICTIONARY (8th ed. 2004).

[3] BRYAN A. GARNER, A DICTIONARY OF MODERN LEGAL USAGE (1990).

[4] *See, e.g.*, FED. R. EVID. 803(19), 803(21).

[5] Luis M.B. Cabral, *The Economics of Trust and Reputation: A Primer* (June 2005 draft), *http://pages.stern.nyu.edu/~lcabral/reputation/ReputationJune05.pdf* (treating information about reputation as inputs into Bayesian calculations).

[6] Indeed, this has spurred the formation of an industry association, the Rating and Review Professional Association. *http://www.rarpa.org*.

[7] *http://pages.ebay.com/services/forum/feedback.html*.

- Amazon's product reviews, which allows consumers to rate and review millions of marketplace products.
- Yelp.com, which allows consumers to review local businesses.
- TripAdvisor.com, which allows consumers to review hotels and other travel attractions.
- RealSelf.com, which allows consumers to review cosmetic surgery procedures.
- Avvo.com, which allows consumers to rate and review attorneys.
- Glassdoor.com, which allows employees to share salary information and critique the working conditions at their employers.
- Honestly.com,[8] which allows co-workers to review each other.
- RateMyProfessors.com, which allows students to publicly rate and review their professors.
- DontDateHimGirl.com, which allows people to create and "find profiles of men who are alleged cheaters."[9]
- TheEroticReview.com, which allows johns to rank prostitutes.[10]

Why Reputational Information Matters

In theory, the marketplace works through an "invisible hand": consumers and producers make individual and autonomous decisions that, without any centralized coordination, collectively determine the price and quantity of goods and services. When it works properly, the invisible hand maximizes social welfare by allocating goods and services to those consumers who value them the most.

A properly functioning invisible hand also should reward good producers and punish poor ones. Consumers allocating their scarce dollars in a competitive market will transact with producers who provide the best cost or quality options. Over time, uncompetitive producers should be drummed out of the industry by the aggregate but uncoordinated choices of rational and informed consumers.

However, given the transaction costs inherent in the real world, the invisible hand can be subject to distortions. In particular, to the extent information about producers is costly to obtain or use, consumers may lack crucial information to make accurate decisions. To that extent, consumers may not be able to easily compare producers or their price/quality offerings, in which case good producers may not be rewarded and bad producers may not be punished.

When information is costly, reputational information can improve the operation of the invisible hand by helping consumers make better decisions about vendors. In this sense, reputational information acts like an invisible hand guiding the invisible hand (an effect I call the "secondary invisible hand"), because reputational information can guide consumers to make marketplace choices that, in aggregate, effectuate the invisible hand. Thus, in an information economy with transaction costs, reputational information can play an essential role in rewarding good producers and punishing poor ones.

Given this crucial role in marketplace mechanisms, any distortions in reputational information may effectively distort the marketplace itself. In effect, it may cause the secondary invisible hand to push the invisible hand in the wrong direction, allowing bad producers to escape punishment and failing to reward good producers. To avoid this unwanted consequence, any regulation of reputational information needs to be carefully considered to ensure it is improving, not harming, marketplace mechanisms.

Note that the secondary invisible hand is, itself, subject to transaction costs. It is costly for consumers to find and assess the credibility of reputational information. Therefore, reputation systems themselves typically seek to establish their own reputation. I describe the reputation of reputation systems as a "tertiary" invisible hand—it is the invisible hand that guides reputational information (the secondary invisible hand) to guide the invisible hand of individual uncoordinated decisions by marketplace actors (the primary invisible hand). Thus, the tertiary invisible hand allows the reputation system to earn consumer trust as a credible source (such as

---

[8] Honestly.com was previously called Unvarnished. *See* Evelyn Rusli, *Unvarnished: A Clean, Well-Lighted Place For Defamation*, TECHCRUNCH, Mar. 30, 2010, http://techcrunch.com/2010/03/30/unvarnished-a-clean-well-lighted-place-for-defamation/.

[9] PlayerBlock is a similar service, tracking undesirable dating prospects by their cellphone number. *See* Leslie Katz, *Is Your Date a Player? Send a Text and Find Out*, CNET News.com, Oct. 22, 2007, http://news.cnet.com/8301-10784|3-9802025-7.html.

[10] *See* Matt Richtel, *Sex Trade Monitors a Key Figure's Woes*, N.Y. TIMES, June 17, 2008. PunterNet is another website in this category, providing reviews of British sex workers. John Omizek, *PunterNet Thanks Harriet for Massive Upswing*, THE REGISTER, Oct. 5, 2009, http://www.theregister.co.uk/2009/10/05/punternet\harman/.

the *Wall Street Journal,* the *New York Times* or *Consumer Reports*) or to be drummed out of the market for lack of credibility (such as the now-defunct anonymous gossip website JuicyCampus).[11]

Thinking About Reputation Regulation

This part explores some ways that the regulatory system interacts with reputation systems and some issues caused by those interactions.

Regulatory Heterogeneity

Regulators have taken divergent approaches to reputation systems. For example, consider the three different regulatory schemes governing job references, credit reporting databases and consumer review websites:

- Job references are subject to a mix of statutory (primarily state law) and common law tort regulation.
- Credit reporting databases are statutorily micromanaged through the voluminous and detailed Fair Credit Reporting Act.[12]
- Consumer review websites are virtually unregulated, and many potential regulations of consumer review websites (such as defamation) are statutorily preempted.

These different regulatory structures raise some related questions. Are there meaningful distinctions between reputation systems that support heterogeneous regulation? Are there "best practices" we can observe from these heterogeneous regulatory approaches that can be used to improve other regulatory systems? These questions are important because regulatory schemes can significantly affect the efficacy of reputation systems. As an example, consider the differences between the job reference and online consumer review markets.

A former employer giving a job reference can face significant liability whether the reference is positive or negative.[13] Giving unfavorable references of former employees can lead to defamation or related claims;[14] and there may be liability for a former employee giving an incomplete positive reference.[15]

Employers may be statutorily required to provide certain objective information about former employees.[16] Otherwise, given the potentially no-win liability regime for communicating job references, most knowledgeable employers refuse to provide any subjective recommendations of former employees, positive or negative.[17]

To curb employers' tendency towards silence, many states enacted statutory immunities to protect employers from lawsuits over job references.[18] However, the immunities have not changed employer reticence, which has led to a virtual collapse of the job reference market.[19] As a result, due to mis-calibrated regulation, the job reference market fails to provide reliable reputational information.

In contrast, the online consumer review system is one of the most robust reputation systems ever. Millions of consumers freely share their subjective opinions about marketplace goods and services, and consumer review websites keep proliferating.

There are several possible reasons why consumer review websites might succeed where offline reputation systems might fail. My hypothesis, discussed in a companion essay in this collection, is that the difference is partially explained by 47 U.S.C. § 230, passed in 1996—at the height of Internet exceptionalism—to protect online publishers from liability for third party content. Section 230 lets websites collect and organize individual consumer reviews without worrying about crippling legal liability for those reviews. As a result, consumer review websites can motivate consumers to share their opinions and then publish those opinions widely—as deter-

---

[11] Matt Ivester, *A Juicy Shutdown,* JUICYCAMPUS BLOG, Feb. 4, 2009, http://juicycampus.blogspot.com/2009/02/juicy-shutdown.html.
[12] 15 U.S.C. §§ 1681–81x.
[13] *See* Tresa Baldas, *A Rash of Problems over Job References,* NAT'L L.J., Mar. 10, 2008 ("Employers are finding that they are being sued no matter what course they take; whether they give a bad reference, a good reference or stay entirely silent.").
[14] 1–2 EMPLOYMENT SCREENING § 2.05 (Matthew Bender & Co. 2008) (hereinafter "EMPLOYMENT SCREENING").
[15] Randi W. v. Muroc Joint Unified Sch. Dist., 14 Cal. 4th 1066 (1997).
[16] These laws are called "service letter statutes." *See* EMPLOYMENT SCREENING, *supra* note 14. Germany has a mandatory reference law requiring employers to furnish job references, but in response German employers have developed an elaborate system for coding the references. Matthew W. Finkin & Kenneth G. Dau-Schmidt, *Solving the Employee Reference Problem,* 57 AM. J. COMP. L. 387 (2009).
[17] *See* Baldas, *supra* note 13.
[18] The immunizations protect employer statements made in good faith. EMPLOYMENT SCREENING, *supra* note 14.
[19] *See* Finkin & Dau-Schmidt, *supra* note 16.

mined by marketplace mechanisms (*i.e.*, the tertiary invisible hand), not concerns about legal liability.

The success of consumer review websites is especially noteworthy given that individual reviewers face the same legal risks that former employers face when providing job references, such as the risk of personal liability for publishing negative reputational information. Indeed, numerous individuals have been sued for posting negative online reviews.[20] As a result, rational actors should find it imprudent to submit negative reviews; yet, millions of such reviews are published online. A number of theories might explain this discrepancy, but one theory is especially intriguing: Mediating websites, privileged by their own liability immunity, find innovative ways to get consumers over their fears of legal liability.

What lessons can we draw from this comparison? One possible lesson is that reputation systems are too important to be left to the market. In other words, the tertiary invisible hand may not ensure accurate and useful information, or the costs of inaccurate information (such as denying a job to a qualified candidate) may be too excessive. If so, extensive regulatory intervention of reputation systems may improve the marketplace.

An alternative conclusion—and a more convincing one to me—is that the tertiary invisible hand, aided by a powerful statutory immunity like Section 230, works better than regulatory intervention. If so, we may get better results by deregulating reputation systems.

System Configurations

Given the regulatory heterogeneity, I wonder if there is an "ideal" regulatory configuration for reputation systems, especially given the tertiary invisible hand and its salutary effect on publisher behavior. Two brief examples illustrate the choices available to regulators, including the option of letting the marketplace operate unimpeded:

Anti-Gaming. A vendor may have financial incentives to distort the flow of reputational information about it. This reputational gaming can take many forms, including disseminating false positive reports about the vendor,[21] disseminating false negative reports about the vendor's competitors, or manipulating an intermediary's sorting or weighting algorithm to get more credit for positive reports or reduce credit for negative reports. Another sort of gaming can occur when users intentionally flood a reputation system with inaccurate negative reports as a form of protest.[22]

Do regulators need to curb this gaming behavior, or will other forces be adequate? There are several marketplace pressures that curb gaming, including competitors policing each other,[23] just as they do in false advertising cases.[24] In addition, the tertiary invisible hand may encourage reputation systems to provide adequate "policing" against gaming. However, when the tertiary invisible hand is weak, such as with fake blog posts where search engines are the only mediators,[25] government intervention might be worth considering.

Right of Reply. A vendor may wish to publicly respond to reputational information published about it in an immediately adjacent fashion. Many consumer review websites allow vendors to comment or otherwise reply to user-supplied reviews, but not all do. For example, Yelp initially drew significant criticism from business owners who could not effectively reply to negative Yelp reviews because of Yelp's archi-

---

[20] *See, e.g.*, Wendy Davis, *Yelp Reviews Spawn At Least Five Lawsuits*, MEDIAPOST ONLINE MEDIA DAILY, Jan. 21, 2009, *http://www.mediapost.com/publications/?fa=Articles.printFriendly &artlaid=9877 8;* Agard v. Hill, 2010 U.S. Dist. LEXIS 35014 (E.D. Cal. 2010).

[21] Lifestyle Lift Holding, Inc. v. RealSelf Inc., 2:08–cv–10089–PJD–RSW (answer/counterclaims filed March 3, 2008), *http://www.realself.com/files/Answer.pdf* (alleging that Lifestyle Lift posted fake positive reviews about its own business to an online review website).

[22] For example, consumers protesting the digital rights management (DRM) in EA's Spore game flooded Amazon's review site with one-star reviews, even though many of them actually enjoyed the game. *See* Austin Modine, *Amazon Flash Mob Mauls Spore DRM*, THE REGISTER, Sept. 10, 2008, *http://www.theregister.co.uk/2008/09/10/sporeldrmlamazonleffect/*. A similar protest hit Intuit's TurboTax 2008 over its increased prices. *See* Steven Musil, *Amazon Reviewers Slam TurboTax Fee Changes*, CNET NEWS.COM, Dec. 7, 2008, *http://news.cnet.com/8301–1001l3-10117323-92.html.*

[23] *See* Cornelius v. DeLuca, 2010 WL 1709928 (D. Idaho Apr. 26, 2010) (a marketplace vendor sued over alleged shill online reviews posted by competitors).

[24] *See, e.g.*, Lillian R. BeVier, *A Puzzle in the Law of Deception*, 78 VA. L. REV. 1 (1992).

[25] *See* Press Release, New York Office of the Attorney General, Attorney General Cuomo Secures Settlement With Plastic Surgery Franchise That Flooded Internet With False Positive Reviews, July 14, 2009, *http://www.ag.ny.gov/medialcenter/2009/july/july14bl09.html.*

tecture,[26] but Yelp eventually relented and voluntarily changed its policy.[27] As another example, Google permitted quoted sources to reply to news articles appearing in Google News as a way to "correct the record."[28]

Regulators could require consumer review websites and other reputation systems to permit an adjacent response from the vendor.[29] But such intervention may not be necessary; the tertiary invisible hand can prompt reputation systems to voluntarily provide a reply option (as Yelp and Google did) when they think the additional information helps consumers.

Undersupply of Reputational Information

There are three primary categories of reasons why reputational information may be undersupplied.

Inadequate Production Incentives

Much reputational information starts out as non-public (*i.e.*, "private") information in the form of a customer's subjective mental impressions about his/her interactions with the vendor. To the extent this information remains non-public, it does not help other consumers make marketplace decisions. These collective mental impressions represent a vital but potentially underutilized social resource.

The fact that non-public information remains locked in consumers' heads could represent a marketplace failure. If the social benefit from public reputational information exceeds the private benefit from making it public, then presumptively there will be an undersupply of public reputational information. If so, the government may need to correct this failure by encouraging the disclosure of reputational information—such as by creating a tort immunity for sites that host that disclosure, as Section 230 does, or perhaps by going further. But there already may be market solutions to this problem, as evidenced by the proliferation of online review websites eliciting lots of formerly non-public reputational information.

Further, relatively small amounts of publicly disclosed reputational information might be enough to properly steer the invisible hand. For example, the first consumer review of a product in a reputation system creates a lot of value for subsequent consumers, but the 1,000th consumer review of the same product may add very little incrementally. So even if most consumer impressions remain non-public, perhaps mass-market products and vendors still have enough information produced to keep them honest. At the same time, vendors and products in the "long tail"[30] may have inadequate non-public impressions put into the public discourse, creating a valuable opportunity for comprehensive reputation systems to fix the omission. However, reputation systems will tackle these obscure marketplace options only when they can keep their costs low (given that consumer interest and traffic will, by definition, be low), and reputation system deregulation helps reduce both the costs of litigation as well as responding to takedown demands.

Vendor Suppression of Reputational Information

Vendors are not shy about trying to suppress unwanted consumer reviews ex post,[31] but vendors might try to suppress such reviews ex ante. For example, one café owner grew so tired of negative Yelp reviews that he put a "No Yelpers" sign in his café's windows.[32]

That sign probably had no legal effect, but Medical Justice offers an ex ante system to help doctors use preemptive contracts to suppress reviews by their patients. Medical Justice provides doctors with a form agreement that has patients waive

---

[26] See Claire Cain Miller, *The Review Site Yelp Draws Some Outcries of Its Own*, N.Y. TIMES, Mar. 3, 2009.

[27] *See* Claire Cain Miller, *Yelp Will Let Businesses Respond to Web Reviews*, N.Y. TIMES, Apr. 10, 2009.

[28] *See* Dan Meredith & Andy Golding, *Perspectives About the News from People in the News*, GOOGLE NEWS BLOG, Aug. 7, 2007, http://googlenewsblog.blogspot.com/2007/08/perspectives-about-news-from-people-in.html.

[29] *See* Frank A. Pasquale, *Rankings, Reductionism, and Responsibility*, 54 CLEV. ST. L. REV. 115 (2006); Frank A. Pasquale, *Asterisk Revisited: Debating a Right of Reply on Search Results*, 3 J. BUS. & TECH. L. 61 (2008).

[30] Chris Anderson, *The Long Tail*, WIRED, Oct. 2004, http://www.wired.com/wired/archive/12.10/tail.html.

[31] *See* Eric Goldman, *Online Word of Mouth and Its Implications for Trademark Law*, in TRADEMARK LAW AND THEORY: A HANDBOOK OF CONTEMPORARY RESEARCH 404 (Graeme B. Dinwoodie and Mark D. Janis eds.) (2008) (discussing lopsided databases where all negative reviews are removed, leaving only positive reviews).

[32] Stefanie Olsen, *No Dogs, Yelpers Allowed*, CNET NEWS.COM, Aug. 14, 2007, http://news.cnet.com/8301-10784\3-9759933-7.html.

their rights to post online reviews of the doctor.[33] Further, to bypass 47 U.S.C. § 230s protective immunity for online reputation systems that might republish such patient reviews, the Medical Justice form prospectively takes copyright ownership of any patient-authored reviews.[34] (Section 230 does not immunize against copyright infringement). This approach effectively allows doctors—or Medical Justice as their designee—to get reputation systems to remove any unwanted patient reviews simply by sending a DMCA takedown notice.[35]

Ex ante customer gag orders may be illegal. In the early 2000s, the New York Attorney General challenged software manufacturer Network Associates' end user license agreement, which said the "customer will not publish reviews of this product without prior consent from Network Associates, Inc." In response, the New York Supreme Court enjoined Network Associates from restricting user reviews in its end user license agreement.[36] Medical Justice's scheme may be equally legally problematic.

From a policy standpoint, ex ante customer gag orders pose serious threats to the invisible hand. If they work as intended, they starve reputation systems of the public information necessary to facilitate the marketplace. Therefore, regulatory efforts might be required to prevent ex ante customer gag orders from wreaking havoc on marketplace mechanisms.

Distorted Decision-Making from Reputational Information

Reputational information generally improves decision-making, but not always. Most obviously, reputational information relies on the accuracy of past information in predicting future behavior, but this predictive power is not perfect.

First, marketplace actors are constantly changing and evolving, so past behavior may not predict future performance. For example, a person with historically bad credit may obtain a well-paying job that puts him or her on good financial footing. Or, in the corporate world, a business may be sold to a new owner with different management practices. In these situations, the predictive accuracy of past information is reduced.[37]

Second, some past behavior may be so distracting that information consumers might overlook other information that has more accurate predictive power. For example, a past crime or bankruptcy can overwhelm the predictive information in an otherwise-unblemished track record of good performance.

Ultimately, a consumer of information must make smart choices about what information to consult and how much predictive weight to assign to that information. Perhaps regulation can improve the marketplace's operation by shaping the information that consumers consider. For example, if some information is so highly prejudicial that it is likely to distort consumer decision-making, the marketplace might work better if we suppress that information from the decision-maker.[38]

At the same time, taking useful information out of the marketplace could create its own adverse distortions of the invisible hand. Therefore, we should tread cautiously in suppressing certain categories of information.

Conclusion

Although "reputation" has been extensively studied in a variety of social science disciplines, there has been comparatively little attention paid to how regulation affects the flow of reputational information in our economy. Understanding these dynamics would be especially valuable in light of the proliferation of Internet-mediated reputation systems and the irresistible temptation to regulate novel and innovative reputation systems based on emotion, not necessarily sound policy considerations.

---

[33] Lindsey Tanner, *Doctors Seek Gag Orders to Stop Patients' Online Reviews*, ASSOCIATED PRESS, Mar. 3, 2009, http://www.usatoday.com/news/health/2009-03-05-doctor-reviews\N .htm.

[34] Michael E. Carbine, *Physicians Use Copyright Infringement Threat to Block Patient Ratings on the Web*, AIS'S HEALTH BUSINESS DAILY, Mar. 30, 2009, http://www.aishealth.com/Bnow/hbd033009.html.

[35] 17 U.S.C. § 512(c)(3).

[36] People v. Network Associates, Inc., 758 N.Y.S.2d 466 (N.Y. Sup. Ct. 2003).

[37] *Cf.* Note, *Badwill*, 116 HARV. L. REV. 1845 (2003) (describing how companies can mask a track record of bad performance through corporate renaming).

[38] *Cf.* FED. R. EVID. 403 ("Although relevant, evidence may be excluded if its probative value is substantially outweighed by the danger of unfair prejudice, confusion of the issues, or misleading the jury . . ."). This fear underlies a French proposal to enact a "right to forget" statute. *See* David Reid, *France Ponders Right-to-Forget Law*, BBC CLICK, Jan. 8, 2010, http://news.bbc.co.uk/2/hi/programmes/click\online/8447742.stm.

PATIENTS' ONLINE REVIEWS OF PHYSICIANS

By Eric Goldman*

Medical Ethics, A JOURNAL PUBLISHED BY LAHEY HEALTH FALL 2013, PAGE 6

Online patient reviews are becoming a major force in the healthcare industry, but some healthcare providers lament this development. In fact, an opportunistic vendor, Medical Justice, preyed on healthcare provider fears and sold healthcare providers a form contract that asked patients to waive their rights to post reviews. Medical Justice eventually recognized the errors of that approach and did a complete reversal; it is now selling healthcare providers a service, eMerit, that monitors search engines and doctor rating sites.

Medical Justice's contracts prohibiting online reviews have not been definitively tested in court, but attempts to restrict patient reviews are problematic. Anti-review contracts prevent consumers from expressing their views, and they deprive other consumers of information that can help them make better marketplace choices. The provisions also create serious legal risks for the businesses imposing them, as illustrated by the following three incidents:

- In the late 1990s, software company Network Associates restricted buyers from publishing reviews of its software. In 2003, a New York court enjoined Network Associates from continuing to use that restriction.[1]
- The U.S. Department of Health and Human Service's Office of Civil Rights required a doctor to stop using Medical Justice's anti-review form.[2] The agreement prohibited the patient from "directly or indirectly publishing or airing commentary about the physician, his expertise, and/or treatment in exchange for the physician's compliance with the Privacy Rule."
- New York dentist Stacey Makhnevich and her practice Aster Dental required that patients sign a Medical Justice–based confidentiality agreement as a precondition to treatment. This version of the agreement tried to silence patients by assigning to the dentists a copyright over any comments related to their treatment. The patient, Robert Lee, had a dental emergency and signed the agreement to get treatment. He later sued to invalidate the agreement. The court's initial opinion signaled serious skepticism about the legitimacy of the dentist's conduct.[3]

Even more important than the legal risks, asking patients to restrict their rights to review a healthcare provider sends a terrible message to patients and sets the stage for distrust.

While contractually restricting patients' reviews is not the right answer, some healthcare providers are frustrated by their perceived inability to publicly defend themselves from negative patient reviews. Providers have ethical and legal obligations to maintain patient confidentiality, with severe penalties for noncompliance. These restrictions seemingly impose a gag order on doctors to rebut patient misstatements.

If a patient's review misstates facts, healthcare providers actually have several options:

- A patient may consent to discussing the matter publicly. Angie's List prospectively requires this consent from patients who review doctors.[4]
- Most patients' criticisms of their healthcare provider don't relate to individualized medical advice. As one recent study found, "Unhappy patients who post negative online reviews of their doctors complain about poor customer service and bedside manner four times more often than misdiagnoses and inadequate

---

*Professor and Director of High Tech Law Institute, Santa Clara University School of Law. egoldman@gmail.com. http://www.ericgoldman.org.
[1] New York v. Network Associates, Inc., 758 N.Y.S.2d 466 (N.Y. Sup. Ct. 2003).
[2] *Health Information Privacy: Private Practice Ceases Conditioning of Compliance with the Privacy Rule*, US Dept of Health & Human Services, Office of Civil Rights, Health Information Privacy: Private Practice Ceases Conditioning of Compliance with the Privacy Rule, http://www.hhs.gov/ocr/privacy/hipaa/enforcement/examples/allcases.html#case29.
[3] Lee v. Makhnevich, 2013 WL 1234829 (S.D.N.Y. March 27, 2013).
[4] Angie's List Membership Agreement, April 25, 2012, § 13, http://my.angieslist.com/angieslist/aluseragreement.aspx ("You also acknowledge that the healthcare or wellness provider about whom you submit Content may submit Service Provider Content that contain your private or confidential health information in response to Content you submit").

medical skills."[5] If a healthcare provider feels the need to publicly respond, he or she can rebut most of these issues without discussing confidential patient information.

- If patients discuss their specific medical situations, the healthcare provider may discuss its general philosophies and standard protocols without disclosing confidential patient information.

Doctors also can bring lawsuits to redress negative patient reviews, but litigation isn't a great option. There is no point in suing online review websites for patient reviews. Review websites are categorically protected from liability for third-party content except in cases involving intellectual property (see 47 U.S.C. § 230). No doctor has ever successfully won in court against an online review website for publishing patient reviews.

Suing patients is only marginally more attractive than suing review websites, even if a patient has lied. Inevitably the patient will respond with a malpractice claim or a complaint against a provider's license; a lawsuit calls more attention to the patient's assertions; doctors suing patients often look like they have something to hide; and, perhaps most importantly, doctors are not likely to win in court.

Over the past decade, I've identified about two dozen doctor vs. patient lawsuits over online reviews. Doctors have rarely won against their patients in court and, even worse, some doctors have been ordered to pay their patients' attorneys' fees.[6]

The legal analysis is more complicated if it can be proven that a competitor or vindictive party is posting fake reviews. Those lawsuits are more winnable than lawsuits against patients, but often the time and costs required to win simply aren't worth it.

Online patient reviews remain a work-in-progress; more work needs to be done, especially on the part of review websites, to improve the credibility of patient reviews. Still, online patient reviews are good news to the healthcare industry, not bad news. Patient reviews will improve the industry's service levels, providing valuable customer feedback to healthcare providers and help them improve their service. Good healthcare providers will be recognized for the quality services they provide.

The CHAIRMAN. Thank you very much, Professor Goldman. Mr. Rheingold?

STATEMENT OF IRA RHEINGOLD, EXECUTIVE DIRECTOR, NATIONAL ASSOCIATION OF CONSUMER ADVOCATES

Mr. RHEINGOLD. Thank you, Mr. Chairman Thune, Ranking Member Nelson, and members of the Committee.

This morning, I would like to make three points:

One, no one who has been paying attention over the past decades, as consumer rights have been slowly stripped away through often unseen form contracts, should be surprised by the presence and growth of non-disparagement or "gag" clauses.

Two, the idea behind the legislation crafted to solve this problem is a good one and fits into the long history of legislative action designed to not only protect consumers but also our market economy.

And, three, as of now, we are unable to support this bill because it seeks to limit the enforcement rights of State and Federal officials.

When I see non-disparagement clauses, I unfortunately see the logical conclusion of a decades-long corporate effort to strip consumers of yet another fundamental right. Buried in fine print, consumers today are typically required to waive all sorts of rights, including the right to seek relief in our public justice system and now, with these "gag clauses," the right to even speak.

---

[5] Press Release: *Online Doctor Reviews: Four Times More Patients Peeved About Service & Bedside Manner Than Medical Skills,* April 30, 2013, *http://www.reuters.com/article/2013/04/30/idUSnGNX736vBG+1c3+GNW20130430.*

[6] See the complete chart at *http://digitalcommons.law.scu.edu/cgi/viewcontent.cgi?article=1289&context=historical.*

What is happening is obvious. Through the use of indecipherable language and non-negotiable form contracts, corporations have first successfully stripped consumers of their Seventh Amendment right to a jury trial. Why should we be surprised when corporations want to do the same to the consumers' First Amendment right of free speech?

In my early years as an attorney, I would have believed that these clauses that waive fundamental constitutional rights would have been deemed unconscionable and unenforceable. Surely, there was no consent by the consumer. Surely, it was unconscionable for powerful businesses to deny consumers the right to tell their story in our public courts. Surely, if we proved that these clauses prevent consumers from getting legal help, from getting proper redress, they would be unenforceable. Surely, I would be wrong.

While I was wrong in expecting courts, particularly the Supreme Court, from stopping businesses from stripping a fundamental right from consumers, I—we—should not repeat that mistake. Therefore, Congress should pass a bill that prohibits ''gag clauses,'' as well as pass the Arbitration Fairness Act.

Simply, these ''gag clauses'' attack the very heart of a fair and functioning American marketplace by prohibiting consumers from exercising the freedom of sharing their thoughts and opinions with other consumers.

Consumer protection laws in a free economy protect the market itself and all of its participants. Congress and State legislatures have recognized this fact on countless occasions and have passed a wide variety of laws on these very grounds.

The FTC Act and its progeny, State UDAP laws, were created with the understanding that our market economy would not function properly if unscrupulous businesses were allowed to profit from unfair and deceptive trade practices and inevitably gain competitive advantages over honest businesses.

Federal and State disclosure regimes, like the Truth in Lending Act, exist in large part because of our understanding that a fair and functioning marketplace is dependent on consumers making informed and knowledgeable decisions.

The Fair Credit Reporting Act, a law that this committee is intimately familiar with, was passed with the full recognition that credit decisions made on the basis of faulty information, whether by credit grantors or consumers, undermine the vitality of the consumer economy.

The idea of S. 2044 to ban non-disparagement clauses stands in the long line of these fundamental consumer market protection statutes. Our market economy only functions properly when unfair practices are exposed and consumers do not make decisions based on faulty information but, instead, when all information, whether disclosed by law or shared by others, is made available for consumers to use and/or ignore in their decisionmaking process.

While protections as proposed in S. 2044 are essential for our consumer marketplace to function fairly and efficiently, its mere passage is not nearly enough to ensure that the rule of law is complied with. Strong enforcement of these statutes by public regulators or by private consumers is essential for laws to have their full effect.

Attorneys General across this country have done yeoman's work in enforcing State and Federal consumer protections. With limited and ever-shrinking budgets and small and ever-shrinking staffs, these important public servants have sought ways to maximize their ability to protect their state's citizens and their state's economy.

Their efforts, including collectively working across state lines in a bipartisan manner, have been essential in obtaining justice for consumers far beyond what might be possible if their work was limited to what was achievable by their own limited staff and advocacy tools.

Similarly, the partnership that some Attorneys General have formed with experienced and capable private attorneys, particularly in instances when they are attempting to enforce the law against big and deep-pocketed corporations, has led to a measure of justice and consumer relief otherwise completely unattainable.

Simply, if we want Attorneys General to enforce the law, Congress should not limit these state officials from choosing how they best can protect consumers in their own state.

We fully support the idea behind S. 2044. There is no place in the American economy for denying consumers like Jen Palmer the right to speak freely about their experiences in the consumer marketplace. However, for a consumer market protection statute to be fully effective, it must be fully enforceable.

Because this bill limits the ability of public regulators from using all of their necessary enforcement tools, we cannot currently support it. If this provision is removed from the bill, we would be pleased in offering our full support for this important legislative effort.

Thank you.

[The prepared statement of Mr. Rheingold follows:]

PREPARED STATEMENT OF IRA RHEINGOLD, EXECUTIVE DIRECTOR, NATIONAL ASSOCIATION OF CONSUMER ADVOCATES

Mr. Chairman Thune, Ranking Member Nelson, and Members of the Committee, thank you for inviting me to testify today about "non-disparagement clauses," and why these contract terms do great harm, not only to consumers, but to honest and ethical businesses attempting to compete in the consumer marketplace.

I offer my testimony today as the Executive Director of the National Association of Consumer Advocates (NACA). NACA is a non-profit organization whose members are private and public sector attorneys, legal services attorneys, law professors, and law students, whose primary focus involves the protection and representation of consumers.

In my testimony, I will first talk about the importance of consumer protection laws, not just as a means to shield consumers from bad business behavior, but as market protection statutes that allow honest businesses to compete on a level playing field. Next, I'll look at the consumer "gag" clauses that are a focus of this hearing, in the context of a decades-long effort by corporations to hide their conduct from public scrutiny through the fine print of form contracts. Finally, I'll explain that while we are very pleased that the Senate is taking up this very issue, we are unable to support S. 2044 in its present form because it seeks to limit the enforcement rights of state and Federal officials.

1. Consumer Protection is Marketplace Protection

As someone who has been a consumer advocate for almost thirty years, I am often dismayed at the misperception, as well as the battles fought over the need for both creation and enforcement of strong consumer protection laws. Simply, consumer protection laws are market protection laws. They do not merely protect consumers, they also protect honest businesses.

Consumer protection laws in a free market economy by definition protect the market itself and all of its participants. The Supreme Court stated the guiding principle of this philosophy nearly 40 years ago: "[B]lind economic activity is inconsistent with the efficient functioning of a free economic system such as ours." *Mourning v. Family Publication Serv., Inc.*, 411 U.S. 356, 364 (1973). Congress and state legislatures have recognized this fact on countless occasions and have passed a wide variety of laws on these very grounds. The FTC Act and its progeny, state Unfair and Deceptive Acts and Practices laws were created with the understanding that our market economy would not function properly if unscrupulous businesses were allowed to profit from unfair and deceptive trade practices and inevitably gain competitive advantages over honest businesses. Federal and state disclosure regimes, like the Truth in Lending Act, exist in large part because of our understanding that a fair and functioning marketplace is dependent on consumers making informed and knowledgeable decisions. The Fair Credit Reporting Act, a statute that this committee is intimately familiar, was passed with the full recognition that credit decisions made on the basis of faulty information, whether by credit grantors or consumers, undermine the vitality of the consumer economy.

S. 2044—looking past its serious flaw of limiting enforcement of the very protections it hopes to create (which I will address below)—stands in the long line of these fundamental consumer/market place protection statutes. Simply, our market economy only functions properly, when unfair practices are exposed and consumers do not make decisions based on faulty information, but instead all information—whether disclosed by law or shared by others—is made available for consumers to use and/or ignore in their decision making process.

2. Non-Disparagement Clauses—just another attempt to strip consumers of a fundamental right

When I look at non-disparagement clauses—a contract term designed to prevent consumers from freely expressing a negative opinion about a business—being imposed on consumers by a "form" contract, by the click of a button, or by the mere notice on a web page, I simply see the logical conclusion of a decades long corporate effort to strip consumers of yet another fundamental right.

Buried in the fine print of everything from consumer "contracts," including credit cards, cell phones, car purchase, student loans, and new homes, to employee handbooks and nursing home admissions contracts, consumers are typically required to waive all sorts of rights, including the right to hold businesses liable for their bad acts, to enforce consumer protection statutes, to gain access to our public justice system, and now even the right to speak. The trend is obvious. Through the use of indecipherable language in non-negotiable form contracts and in unnoticed disclaimers, corporations have successfully stripped consumers of their 7th Amendment right to a jury trial. Why should we be surprised when corporations want to do the same to consumers' 1st Amendment right of free speech?

The parallel between denying consumers a public day in court to denying their right to speak out is undeniable. Like non-disparagement clauses, pre-dispute binding mandatory arbitration clauses force consumers to surrender a fundamental right. Forced arbitration terms, like non-disparagement clauses, are designed to keep complaints private, out of view of the public and the press. In the same way both types of clauses limit the ability of consumers to hold corporate wrongdoers accountable and does damage to both honest businesses and our market economy by limiting the information available to consumers attempting to make informed choices.

During the first half of my professional life, I represented clients in some of the poorest communities in our country and for the last 14 years, I have been the executive director of NACA, spending each of my days working with and talking to private and public attorneys deeply committed to seeking justice for the least powerful consumers. In my early years as an attorney, I would have believed that these "contract" clauses—that waive fundamental constitutional rights—would have been deemed unconscionable and unenforceable.

Unfortunately, my early naiveté has been worn away by having borne witness to the relentless—and all too often successful effort—of powerful corporations to strip away fundamental consumer rights from those far less powerful. Whether it's been through deregulation, preemption, defunding or ultimately through unconscionable contract terms, the goal and the result has been the same. Avoid corporate accountability by taking power away from anyone who might have the ability to actually hold them accountable for misconduct.

Years ago, when I saw my first arbitration clause in a consumer contract, I gave it little thought.

Surely there was no consent by my client;

Surely it was unconscionable for powerful businesses to deny my clients the right to tell their story in our public courts;

Surely my clients right to join with others in a class action—a right established by state law and Federal rule—could not be taken away by an indecipherable form contract, a mere click of a button, or an unread bill stuffer;

Surely, if we proved—as we have—that forced arbitration prevents consumers from getting legal help, from getting proper redress, the clause would be unenforceable;

Surely I would be wrong . . .

While I was wrong in expecting the courts—particularly the Supreme Court—from stopping corporations from stripping a fundamental right from consumers, I/we should not repeat that mistake. Therefore, Congress should pass a bill that prohibits "non-disparagement" clauses, as well as pass the Arbitration Fairness Act[1]. These proposals would restore critical rights and help level the playing field for both consumers and businesses.

3. Why Non Disparagement Clauses should be banned

As I discussed earlier, a fair and functioning marketplace is dependent on consumers making informed and knowledgeable decisions, and using their right to speak publicly to share their views and assist other consumers. Their ability to speak out publicly and to seek accountability facilitates an open and thriving marketplace. Non-disparagement clauses go to the heart of this fundamental principle by prohibiting consumers from exercising the freedom of sharing their thoughts and opinions with other consumers in the American marketplace. Today, in our modern and interconnected economy, this information sharing is even more essential than ever before.

I know for myself, I can no longer decide to go to a restaurant with my family without one of my sons searching Yelp for the latest consumer reviews and ratings. Other family decisions, whether it's buying a car (Consumer Reports), a bathroom vanity (Costco), taking a vacation (TripAdvisor) or booking a hotel (too many to name) are all informed by reading reviews provided by previous customers. Simply, the presence and growth of non-disparagement clauses would prevent the marketplace from working as it should for most American consumers.

This limitation on the fundamental right of free speech as well as the impact it would have on the American market as we know it should be grounds enough from banning the imposition of non-disparagement clauses. Yet, these clauses should also be banned because companies should not have the power to threaten and punish consumers who want to express their criticism of a product; and companies should not have the power to retaliate against consumers who don't act as a company demands. Further, a law barring non-disparagement clauses would publicly declare that non-negotiated form contracts cannot and should not be used to take away fundamental American rights.

4. Attorneys General should have full enforcement authority

As I discussed above, and as Congress has repeatedly recognized, consumer/market protection statutes as proposed in S. 2044 are essential for our consumer marketplace to function fairly and efficiently. But the mere existence of these statutes is not nearly enough to ensure that the rule of law is complied with. Strong enforcement of those statutes—by public regulators or by private consumers—is essential for laws to have their full effect.

Attorneys General across this country have, over the past decades, done yeoman's work in enforcing state and Federal consumer protections. With limited—and ever shrinking budgets—and small—and ever shrinking staffs, these important public servants have sought ways to maximize their ability to protect their state's citizens and their state's economy. Their efforts—including collectively working across state lines in a bi-partisan manner-have been essential in obtaining justice for consumers far beyond what might be possible if their work was limited to what was achievable by their own limited staff and advocacy tools.

Similarly, the partnership that some attorneys general have formed with experienced and capable private attorneys—particularly in instances when they are attempting to enforce the law against big and deep pocketed corporations (like mortgage servicers who break the law)—has led to a measure of justice and consumer relief for harm caused by wrongdoing otherwise completely unattainable. Simply, if

---

[1] For a full exploration of the damage done by Forced Arbitration clauses, see the *New York Times* series, "Beware the Fine Print," published November 1–3.

we want attorneys general to enforce the law—Congress should not limit these state officials from choosing how they best can protect consumers in their own state.

5. Conclusion

We fully support the idea behind S. 2044, the Consumer Review Freedom Act of 2015. There is no place in the American economy for denying consumers, like Jen Palmer, the right to speak freely about their experiences in the consumer marketplace. However, for a consumer/market protection statute to be fully effective, it must be fully enforceable. Because this bill limits the ability of public regulators from using all of their necessary enforcement tools we cannot currently support it. If this provision is removed from the bill, we would be pleased in offering our full support for this important legislative effort.

The CHAIRMAN. Thank you, Mr. Rheingold. We appreciate very much your comments on the legislation, and, obviously, we will take into consideration your thoughts as we continue to shape it while it moves through the process.

I wanted to start with 5-minute rounds of questions, and I will start.

Ms. Palmer, you have been through a harrowing ordeal before finally winning in court. Most people would have given up, but you persisted and kept fighting. And, even now, to come across the country to share your story with us today, the experience that you had, speaks volumes about your commitment to this issue.

So why have you continued to stay engaged, as you have, on this issue?

Ms. PALMER. As I said, the only two things we ever wanted to have happen was for my husband's credit to be cleaned so that we could move on with our lives as we had originally planned, and we really did want to make sure that this never happened to anybody else ever again.

When I first contacted the media, I hoped that if our story got out there, other people would be inspired to come forward and say, hey, these people are doing this to me too; what can I do to stop it?

We never dreamed it would come this far. We really didn't. I am so pleased that you are looking at pushing through legislation on a Federal level. I am happy to do anything I can to assist that.

The CHAIRMAN. Well, we appreciate you. Your story has gotten out there.

You testified today that one of the purposes of these gag clauses is to bully and to intimidate consumers into removing negative reviews. And, in your testimony, you described how KlearGear's demand for $3,500 shocked and scared you.

I guess I am wondering if your experience with KlearGear has given you pause about posting reviews for other products.

Ms. PALMER. Absolutely not. Absolutely not. I continue to post reviews for both companies that have given wonderful service and great products to let other consumers know, yes, you should definitely buy from this company, they are wonderful, and also for companies that maybe fell short of the mark and didn't provide such a great product. That information is just as important as the good review.

The CHAIRMAN. OK. Good. Well, I guess after what you experienced with KlearGear, it couldn't get any worse, right?

Ms. PALMER. I would hope not.

The CHAIRMAN. Mr. Medros, TripAdvisor has taken steps to inform its users when a company employs gag clauses. And, on the other side of the equation, I might add, Amazon recently sued a number of companies that allegedly facilitate fake reviews online.

Do you see other large Internet companies taking measures to clean up online reviews to make sure that consumers are getting accurate and authentic information?

Mr. MEDROS. Absolutely.

Before I answer that, let me first, again, thank you for inviting us and for pushing this legislation forward. We think it is incredibly important legislation.

Without a doubt, we see businesses in the hospitality industry attempt to silence critics of their services, and this plays out across a number of other industries. You mentioned the Amazon case. We have seen it with Yelp, in trying to bully Yelp reviewers or other reviewers to remove their comments, to reduce the severity of their comments, or to outright bury those comments with other content, more positive comments.

The CHAIRMAN. OK.

Professor Goldman, I thought you made a great point in your testimony when discussing how consumer reviews make markets stronger and more efficient because they help guide consumers to the best products or services.

To what degree do you think that gag clauses may be distorting the market? And do you think that most consumers are aware of that, that it is going on?

Mr. GOLDMAN. I think that the contract clauses are only a small part of a much larger problem. There are so many disincentives for consumers to share their opinions and perspectives about the businesses that they deal with, and each of those becomes a friction point or a wedge in their willingness to share.

Ms. Palmer here said here proudly that she hasn't been bullied off of the Internet with her reviews, but most consumers don't have the fortitude and confidence that she has. Gag clauses are just one way that businesses can threaten consumers to get them to not only stifle themselves but to remove their legitimate views once they have been posted.

There are some other tools that companies use, as well—for example, threatening defamation and simply saying, "We are going to sue you and take you to court if you don't remove it." And that is why I would also call your attention to things like the Federal anti-SLAPP law that has been considered. That would be another tool to protect consumers from having their legitimate reviews driven off the Internet.

The CHAIRMAN. OK.

My time has expired, so I will turn to Senator Nelson.

Senator NELSON. Ms. Palmer, I am so sorry that you had to go through this experience.

When you went to the TV station and it started getting some publicity, is that when you then decided to go into court? Because you are listed as the plaintiff in *Palmer* v. *KlearGear.*

Ms. PALMER. We had been seeking legal help before we went to the media. I had contacted several lawyers, done a lot of legal research online to find out what my options were. For all the lawyers

I spoke to and said, "Do we have a case?" they said, "Yes, you do. Yes, you do." I said, "Great. Can you represent us?" They said, "Oh, no. We are not touching that with a 10-foot pole." It was so shady and so big, most didn't want to touch it.

It wasn't until after we spoke to the media—I was hoping to find a lawyer that was willing to step forward. And that was when Public Citizen came forward and said, "We can help you. We want to help you. We have the means and resources to do so."

Senator NELSON. Well, that is a good-news story.

Mr. Medros, I want to look at the other side. Tell us about evidence of bad actors trying to take advantage of businesses by threatening to post a false negative complaint.

Mr. MEDROS. There are certainly some instances where consumers threaten a business with a negative review, threaten to share their experience online, and that business, rightfully so, has concern that that is going to impede their future marketing efforts, impede their future business.

But the reality is, first of all, we encourage businesses to proactively communicate those threats to us, and we then monitor those properties for the instance of those negative reviews. In the vast majority of cases, those negative reviews never appear; they are empty threats.

Second, one of the tenets of TripAdvisor is to allow the businesses to respond to any consumer review. So we believe that transparency will solve this problem. Consumers write their reviews, businesses get to respond, and future consumers get to read those responses, the back-and-forth between those two parties, and make their own decision, weigh their own beliefs about whether or not this is the right business for them to visit.

Senator NELSON. OK.

Mr. MEDROS. Overall, this is not a large problem.

Senator NELSON. So you encourage those businesses, if there is a false review, to contact you.

Would this legislation prevent a business owner who is threatened with a false or malicious review from bringing a case in court against the consumer for defamation?

Mr. MEDROS. I am not probably the best person to answer from a legal standpoint.

What I can tell you is that I don't believe it will prevent businesses from interacting with TripAdvisor and asking reviews to be reviewed. We do employ an entire staff, and we look at every review where an owner or another member of our community flags it as inappropriate, against our guidelines, or perhaps irrelevant.

Senator NELSON. At the end of the day, I think what we want is the access to the courts for whoever is the aggrieved party, the consumer or the business. And, in the case of Ms. Palmer, apparently, it was her access to the court that finally brought about the redress of her terrible situation.

Mr. Rheingold, let me ask you, on the arbitration clauses, when Fiat Chrysler recently used this friends-and-family program to basically trade away the right to go into court in exchange for a $200 discount, should we be doing something to protect consumers from more than just the non-disparagement clauses?

Mr. RHEINGOLD. Oh, absolutely. I think you have made a very good point, Senator. The fact is that the consumers can seek redress is through our public courts system.

A lot of these stories and a lot of the bad damages that are done to consumers if they don't have access to the courts—Ms. Palmer was lucky her story was a very compelling story and the press picked it up right away. Sometimes you need to go to court and publicize those stories in ways.

So what Fiat did in that instance is happening across this country in every consumer place that you can imagine—employers, consumers. And it has gotten sanctioned. What is interesting about the Fiat case is there is actually a reward for signing it away. In most instances, people are signing away their right to go to court without ever knowing about it. It has been in clauses, it is in shrink wrap, click-on things.

Arbitration clauses are everywhere in our economy today, and there really is a dual justice system happening right now where consumers don't have access to our courts whenever they reach an agreement or enter into any sort of agreement with any type of business.

Senator NELSON. This committee has seen a proliferation of these things just recently. Fiat Chrysler is just one example, the GM ignition switches and so forth. And now the Takata airbags, that is still in the news, as a matter of fact, today.

And so thank you for your comments, because these things that are subject to mandatory arbitration or adhesion, you would really lose a lot of your ability if we cut off the access for either the aggrieved or the aggrievor into the courts.

Thank you, Mr. Chairman.

The CHAIRMAN. Thank you, Senator Nelson.

And the bill does, by the way, to your point, specifically say that defamation cases, if something said is untrue, those cases can proceed. We don't do anything to impinge on that right.

Senator McCaskill, Senator Blunt, and Senator Moran are still basking in the glory of the Kansas City Royals World Series victory.

Senator MCCASKILL. Yes, we had hardly anybody show up for the party yesterday.

The CHAIRMAN. I noticed that everybody in Kansas and Missouri was there, which begs the question about what you guys were doing here.

Senator MCCASKILL. Well, there aren't that many people in Kansas, so it was basically Missouri, right, Senator Moran?

Senator MORAN. Mr. Chairman, first of all, I would point out that I tried to have a bet with the Senator from New York, and the offer was I would offer Kansas City barbecue if he would agree not to talk for 45 minutes.

[Laughter.]

Senator MORAN. He accepted your bet, not mine.

Senator MCCASKILL. Yes.

Senator MORAN. And, second, every——

Senator MCCASKILL. That was a bad move on your part, considering who it was.

Senator MORAN.—every Kansan is a Royals fan, and many Missourians have another loyalty elsewhere in their state. And, finally, Senator Blunt and I are wearing blue, and you are wearing red.

Senator MCCASKILL. Oh, look at that.

[Laughter.]

Senator MCCASKILL. Oh, my goodness. I won't even go into the history of the team in Kansas City, Missouri. But I will be glad to acknowledge that we are welcoming all the fans from Kansas.

The CHAIRMAN. She is a loyal Cardinal fan, I might add, too, which explains——

Senator MCCASKILL. I am. Both.

The CHAIRMAN.—the color she is wearing.

You are up, Senator McCaskill.

STATEMENT OF HON. CLAIRE McCASKILL, U.S. SENATOR FROM MISSOURI

Senator MCCASKILL. Thank you very much.

I am pleased that Senator Thune has, in an effort to get a bill that we can all agree on, has agreed to take out the provision that limits the tools available to Attorney Generals as it relates to contingency fees.

And let me ask you, Ms. Palmer, I am assuming that there was a contingency agreement with the lawyers that ultimately represented you in this case?

Ms. PALMER. Fortunately, Public Citizen, as a nonprofit, was kind enough to work with us *pro bono* since we really could not afford legal representation on the scale which we needed.

That was the other thing. Aside from people just saying, "We are not touching this," when I said, "Well, what if you just wrote a cease-and-desist letter or just helped us with a little bit?" they were offering thousands of dollars in——

Senator MCCASKILL. Of course. I mean, it is very hard for an individual to get to court——

Ms. PALMER. Absolutely.

Senator MCCASKILL.—unless there is a contingency fee agreement.

Ms. PALMER. Right. And even with the contingencies, they said, "No, we want a retainer." And we said, "If we don't have $3,500 to pay KlearGear, we don't have $5,000 to give to you."

Senator MCCASKILL. Mr. Rheingold?

Mr. RHEINGOLD. Sure. Thank you.

I will admit publicly I am a Chicago Cubs fan, so I am a little disappointed today, but that is OK. Congratulations to Kansas City.

One important thing about consumer statutes is that consumer statutes that Congress has passed, particularly something like the Fair Credit Reporting Act, has fee-shifting provisions. So attorneys who take a case like a fair credit reporting case, like the damage that was done to Ms. Palmer, would not have to charge Ms. Palmer.

So it is not actually a contingency. In fact, what they do is they only get paid if they win that case. And the court will award them damages after they successfully win the case. So it is a little different from contingency.

And the way that Congress has drafted consumer protection statutes in the past, particularly when it comes to private enforcement, is to have those fee-shifting statutes. And that provides the access to consumers when they have been damaged like Ms. Palmer.

Senator MCCASKILL. So did Public Citizen recover the costs, even, of their litigation?

Ms. PALMER. We are still working on tracking KlearGear down to recover any costs.

Senator MCCASKILL. Oh, so you haven't collected yet?

Ms. PALMER. No, ma'am.

Senator MCCASKILL. Are they still in business?

Ms. PALMER. As far as I know, yes.

Senator MCCASKILL. That just drives me crazy.

Ms. PALMER. It should be noted that, in the judgment award, the judge did award us our settlement and tacked on the lawyers' fees for Public Citizen, as well. So if and when anything ever is collected, Public Citizen——

Senator MCCASKILL. Which is the fee shifting that Mr. Rheingold was referring to?

Ms. PALMER. Right.

Senator MCCASKILL. That they have the right to recover their costs.

Ms. PALMER. Right. However, when we were looking——

Senator MCCASKILL. But if you had lost, they wouldn't have gotten anything.

Ms. PALMER. True. And that was always an issue——

Senator MCCASKILL. Right.

Ms. PALMER.—a fear. However, with any of the other lawyers we contacted, they were not interested in working on a contingency basis. They wanted a retainer upfront.

Senator MCCASKILL. And that is one of the challenges, is——

Ms. PALMER. Absolutely.

Senator MCCASKILL.—trying to figure out how we fund lawsuits where there is a legitimate complaint where the damages don't appear to be enough to warrant the risk that a lawyer takes on when they get into the costly litigation.

And that is one of the advantages that these big companies have, is they know that it is small enough—I mean, there are two things a lawyer has to have to bring a lawsuit. One is liability, and the second is damages. And how large the damages are is relevant to whether or not that lawyer wants to take on the costly risk of going forward with a lawsuit, which does kind of even the playing field, I think, in some ways, too much in favor of the big guys.

Let me talk to Mr. Medros about use of service.

Now, I know who drafts this stuff, and they are lawyers. But this is just the terms of service, OK? "Website terms, conditions, and notices." Then this, another five pages of fine print, is privacy.

How many people do you believe are reading that that go on TripAdvisor?

Mr. MEDROS. I would imagine very few people read through the entire terms of use and privacy statement.

Senator MCCASKILL. So what is the point? If we know nobody is reading it, why aren't we working at making this—have you thought about making a stab at making the terms of service as forthcoming and as clear as the rest of your website?

Mr. MEDROS. I think we would welcome the opportunity to make privacy and terms of service clear. We take privacy extremely serious; we take terms of use extremely serious. And giving us the ability to moderate our content according to our guidelines—I believe that, in the case of a bill like this, what you often see is a precedent and a set of standards set for how terms of use and privacy are conveyed to consumers.

Senator MCCASKILL. Yes. You know, one of the reasons adhesion contracts are so successful is because they are buried in a way that the average person is never going to understand what is being done to them.

Mr. MEDROS. Correct.

Senator MCCASKILL. I think many of them would run in horror. I think Ms. Palmer would have run in horror if she would have realized before they ordered those items what that company was purporting to do.

It seems to me that this is something that we really have to work on. Because this is a lot of waste, because nobody is reading this stuff. So why are we doing it if it is not providing the service that it needs to provide to the consumers that it is ostensibly designed for? So we have to work on that.

Thank you, Mr. Chairman.

The CHAIRMAN. Thank you, Senator McCaskill.

And, in your case, Ms. Palmer, too, they added this long after the transaction occurred, correct?

Ms. PALMER. Yes, they did.

I had actually read through the terms of service three times to make sure there was nothing in there that would have prevented me—especially since I didn't purchase the items, my husband did, I wanted to make sure that there wasn't anything preventing me from posting the review versus my husband posting it.

So I did read through it several times. And when they came back at us 3 years later and said, "You violated this non-disparagement clause," I looked at my husband and said, "That didn't exist. There was no non-disparagement clause."

Senator MCCASKILL. Have you thought about going to law school?

[Laughter.]

The CHAIRMAN. Yes. Since you actually read those agreements. That is most impressive, to start with, so yes.

[Laughter.]

The CHAIRMAN. My neighbor to the south, Senator Fischer.

STATEMENT OF HON. DEB FISCHER, U.S. SENATOR FROM NEBRASKA

Senator FISCHER. Thank you, Mr. Chairman.

Professor Goldman, you have mentioned that small businesses, in particular, may make use of these non-disparagement clauses, as many of them view it as personal when they get negative feedback.

I am on the Small Business Committee here in the Senate, and I fully understand how important small businesses are to the state of Nebraska and also to the economy here in our country. So while I agree that the use of these non-disparagement clauses are a practice that should be discouraged, I would like your views on whether this bill contains sufficient, really, protections for small businesses that are out there. Do you think it does?

Mr. GOLDMAN. In the end, the goal is to create a level playing field for small businesses. And so any of their competitors who are distorting their public persona using these anti-review/gag/non-disparagement clauses are actually hurting the overall marketplace and the opportunity for small businesses to go and win over customers to their side of the equation.

So, in fact, if anything, I think this bill is essential for preserving the vitality of the small business community and for making sure that the markets are open for them to come and enter.

Senator FISCHER. And do you think those protections are in this bill?

Mr. GOLDMAN. I would support this bill as it is currently drafted. I did write some thoughts about ways that it could be tweaked, but each of those I think deserves some further discussions. Even if we don't do that, I think this bill would be super-helpful in advancing the interests of small businesses.

Senator FISCHER. Thank you.

And, Mr. Atkinson, do you have any comments about if small businesses—do you believe they are protected under this bill the way it is drafted, where we are still making sure that we allow consumers to be able to express their views without being punished?

Mr. ATKINSON. Yes, I would echo Mr. Goldman's comment that a lot of the damage from these clauses actually are harming some of their small-business competitors who are doing a really good job. Consumers don't have a way to weigh who is better. And so it might hurt a particular small business, but it helps others.

Second, there are still provisions, there are still legal remedies that a company can use if they feel like someone has outright lied. The bill doesn't prohibit a company from taking action in that way.

And, as I said before, you know, there really is a lot of evidence that if small businesses are active, a small-business owner, you know, posts something and says, ''We are concerned about that; we don't agree with the review,'' that it really can minimize the damage if a company is sincere in what they are actually trying to do.

Senator FISCHER. Do you think small businesses, though, have the resources where they would be able to respond to those negative comments, where they really can take action?

It is hard for consumers to take action; we have heard that. It is difficult. Lawsuits are expensive. But what about small businesses on this, as well? How do we reach a balance here?

Mr. ATKINSON. Well, I think the way a lot of the online rating platforms work is you can monitor what people, your customers, are saying about you. And, frankly, in the Internet age, that is something that every business needs to do.

You are not going to search the web every day for everything, but there are platforms that you can and should monitor, as a small-business owner. And, you know, doing that is not, I don't think, overly burdensome, and a quick reply, just, you know, a one-minute kind of reply every once in a while. You know, you don't get negative reviews every day.

So I don't think it is a burden for companies to do that. I think it is actually just good practice now in the Internet age.

Senator FISCHER. OK. Thank you.

Also, Mr. Atkinson, in the Senate version of this bill, we are looking at enforcement of the prohibition on non-disparagement clauses by the Federal Trade Commission, and in the House version, we have the enforcement by the Department of Justice.

Do you have an opinion, one way or the other, on who would be the best-positioned to assume that role?

Mr. ATKINSON. I don't have an opinion on that, but the person who leads this work for us is Daniel Castro, who was not able to be here for flight reasons, and I will talk with him and would be happy to get back with you on that.

Senator FISCHER. OK. That would be great.

Thank you all very much for being here.

The CHAIRMAN. Thank you, Senator Fischer.

Senator Moran?

STATEMENT OF HON. JERRY MORAN, U.S. SENATOR FROM KANSAS

Senator MORAN. Mr. Chairman, thank you very much. Thank you for hosting this hearing and pursuing the concepts contained in this legislation.

On the topic of small business, I would assume that small business actually uses reviews, as well. They are a consumer. Small businesses need information about what business, larger or smaller, that they might want to deal with, and online reviews might be helpful to a small business in making a business decision.

So, while several of you outlined some ideas of how this isn't harmful or perhaps beneficial to small business, one of the other ways is a small business cannot make a mistake. It is more difficult if they enter into an agreement for purchase with another corporation that turns out to be a bad deal. The consequences are greater, harder to recover from.

So I assume that small businesses also utilize the review as they make purchases of goods and services?

I don't know if there is a—everybody is shaking their head. Does anyone want to disagree with that?

OK.

Then, let me ask about state laws. Perhaps this is to the professor. California, I think, in particular, has state laws dealing with—a state law or state laws dealing with this issue?

Mr. GOLDMAN. Yes, California is the only state that has adopted——

Senator MORAN. Others are pursuing or considering that; is that true?

Mr. GOLDMAN. I haven't done a survey——

Senator MORAN. OK.

Mr. GOLDMAN.—of who else is looking at it.

Senator MORAN. Is there anything we could learn from what has transpired—I hate asking this question—anything we could learn from California in the way that——

[Laughter.]

Senator MORAN.—this law has been written or interpreted or enforced?

Mr. GOLDMAN. I don't believe there have been any enforcement actions under the law, so we don't have any data points about how it is actually applying in the field. It is relatively new, so it is early in the process.

The only thing I will call attention to is that there is a statutory damages provision in the California statute that awards consumers who are subjected to these clauses to obtain statutory damages. And I think that is a topic that is worth discussion at this committee, whether that would be a helpful addition to the law.

Senator MORAN. OK.

In addition to that suggestion, let me ask a broader question. While we are focused on non-disparagement clauses, in this world of online reviews, are there other or similar issues that the Commerce Committee, that Congress ought to be paying attention to?

A couple that I think have been mentioned previously, I know have been mentioned previously: fake reviews, false reviews.

Are there issues that surround this new development—certainly, in my life, particularly as a rural small town resident, these reviews occurred. They occurred after church, they occurred at the grocery store, they occurred at the cafe. And people within our community would talk about what service they got or didn't get, how quality the product was or wasn't. Today, I suppose the consequences are just magnified because of the volume of information that is now available.

Is there something we are missing as we only look in this legislation as to this issue of non-disparagement clauses?

Professor Goldman?

Mr. GOLDMAN. If I may, I will reiterate my interest in the Federal anti-SLAPP solution. The idea would be that it would enable lawsuits that are brought alleging defamation or other types of harms like that that are on content that would be of social interest to be tossed early and to fee-shift if they are illegitimate.

And so the real way that reviews get scrubbed off the Internet isn't through these clauses, though these clauses are problematic, but they are because people post them, they are threatened to take them offline, like Ms. Palmer explained. In Ms. Palmer's case, she couldn't remove them, but that was unusual. But in all other cases, when consumers get those threats, the content comes down instantly.

And a Federal anti-SLAPP law would help some consumers decide, "I am not going to be bullied off the Internet, and I won't be betting my house on legal fees that I can defend my interests in court."

Senator MORAN. OK.

Mr. Atkinson?

Mr. ATKINSON. I would just second Mr. Goldman's point on that. ITIF released a report last year on the whole issue of anti-SLAPP and the impact that it has on the Internet economy and commerce. And so we would agree with that. I think that is another component. Obviously, both pieces of the legislation, in our view, are important.

Senator MORAN. Thank you very much.

Mr. Chairman, thank you for this hearing. And I apologize to you for intruding in your commentary on the Royals. It is just nearly impossible not to have the continued Kansas-Missouri battles in the presence of the Senator from Missouri.

[Laughter.]

The CHAIRMAN. I wouldn't have it any other way.

[Laughter.]

The CHAIRMAN. Senator Schatz?

STATEMENT OF HON. BRIAN SCHATZ, U.S. SENATOR FROM HAWAII

Senator SCHATZ. Thank you, Mr. Chairman.

Ms. Palmer, thank you for your courage and your clarity. I know you have been through a lot, and I imagine it has been a difficult several years. We really appreciate everything that you are doing.

Your case perfectly illustrates why we need a law, because individual consumers are in no position to fight this injustice. And your case also shows why we need a Federal law, that a patchwork of individual statutes are not going to work in the age of the Internet.

My first question is for Mr. Atkinson.

We have been talking a little bit about, well, two things, right? One is that consumers don't know what rights they may be waiving as they click "I agree" or as they sign a contract at the hotel desk. And then there is this other question related to intimidation and admonishing or warning customers against a negative online review.

But those are difficult tactical approaches. So which is it that these companies are really employing? Are they tricking customers into signing away their rights, or are they warning customers against a negative online review? Because they can't be doing both at the same time, it seems to me.

Mr. ATKINSON. I think, first of all, there really haven't been enough surveys of this. There are a lot of anecdotes, which I think are quite compelling. We have just heard one here, but then other folks have talked about that. So I think there is a lot there, and we don't know exactly which strategy companies are using more of.

But I think one of the reasons this bill is so important is it is not just the fact that—even if there were no law, if people think that they may be gone after—and I think we are at a point, if we don't solve the problem soon, there could be something in most consumers' minds where it gives them a little bit of doubt, a little bit of fear, "Well, I heard about somebody getting sued; I am just not going to take the risk."

Because if you think about somebody contributing a review, they are actually being a public citizen. They are contributing to the public good. They are taking their valuable time. It is not going to help them. They are trying to help everybody else. And so if we have a sort of collective climate of fear, then people are going to not be able to do it.

Senator SCHATZ. Fair enough. But it does point out that we are operating at the beginning of this problem and, therefore, we are lacking good decision support on exactly the size and scope of the problem.

Speaking of that, does anybody on the panel know primarily whether these clauses are being employed by small or large enterprises? Because it seems to me that that is a pretty important question too.

I would imagine that the reputational risk of a big national or international brand would probably cause bigger companies not to utilize these. But I would like to know whether some of the bigger companies are using them. Does anybody know?

Mr. MEDROS. I don't think TripAdvisor sees any evidence one way or the other. Small businesses up to potentially large businesses what to, in effect, distort consumer opinions online by getting negative reviews withheld in favor of positive reviews.

Senator SCHATZ. Mr. Medros, let me move on to the way TripAdvisor works, in terms of you have essentially a pop-up screen that warns consumers if there is a particular hotel or travel company that has a non-disparagement clause. Is that correct?

Mr. MEDROS. That is correct. We put a badge, a red badge, on the property warning consumers so that they can make an informed decision about whether to stay there knowing that there is a non-disparagement clause.

Senator SCHATZ. How do you figure out whether the company has a non-disparagement clause? Is that based on consumer complaints, or do you have a process internally? Because I would imagine that it is a resource question for you to have a team of lawyers scrubbing all of their individual contracts. So is it just based on, if something pops up, then you notify the public?

Mr. MEDROS. It is based on consumers reporting it to us and then us investigating. And I think that speaks to why, more so than any other reason, we need this legislation. We only see a small percentage of these contracts that may exist. Some consumers may not notice a clause, may be too fearful to report it. And so widespread banishment of these types of clauses are critical for all consumers.

Senator SCHATZ. Well, I think that is the most important point here with respect to whether or not there is a private sector and sort of Internet-based solution. And it seems to me that there is not without a statute, because you just can't make Yelp or TripAdvisor or anybody else responsible for reviewing legal language in any company that may or may not be mentioned on your platform.

Mr. MEDROS. I would wholeheartedly agree. It would be a game of Whac-A-Mole.

Senator SCHATZ. Thank you.

The CHAIRMAN. Thank you, Senator Schatz.

Senator Daines?

STATEMENT OF HON. STEVE DAINES,
U.S. SENATOR FROM MONTANA

Senator DAINES. Thank you, Mr. Chairman. This is a really intriguing subject today.

I spent a number of years with a cloud-computing customer experience solution that we sold. And we were a B2C business, selling to organizations that touched hundreds of thousands, sometimes millions, of consumers.

And it is an overused cliché to suggest that, you know, the customer is in charge. We all know that now, and now it is a cliché in boardrooms because people started to wake up.

But, also, I think, second, is feedback is a gift. And I think it is insecure companies, like bullies on a playground who are insecure, that would have these anti-disparagement clauses. And, you know, welcome to the free markets and the Internet. Let's compete and let the consumer have its voice.

And I think, frankly, it tends to be a bit condescending to consumers to suggest that the consumer—I think consumers can wade through it. They kind of see the folks who are a bit unhinged, perhaps things that are true and aren't false. Let the consumer sort that out is, I guess, my view on it, recognizing there still is a problem with some companies posting false claims to prop it up and competitors posting claims to disparage.

Having said that, I can tell you from Montana's economy viewpoint, tourism is one of our largest businesses. It is $4 billion; 11 million people visit our state. And they are going online, they are booking trips, they are relying on online reviews.

I spoke to a small business owner just a couple weeks ago in kind of an obscure place in Montana. I said, "How was your summer?" He says, "Best summer ever." I said, "Why?" And I was expecting him to say, "We had a big marketing campaign." He said, "Online reviews. People went and they found us."

By the way, Yellowstone National Park has a 4.5 out of 5 rating on Yelp.

[Laughter.]

Senator DAINES. Just a little hometown advertisement there.

Anyway, I guess, though, I am curious about how we ought to approach fake online reviews, if there is a thought on best practices. Whether it is businesses that are paying for positive reviews or competitors who are writing false negative reviews, I am curious if you could share, maybe, some best practices, policies, procedures that you would recommend that should be used to combat fake online reviews.

Please.

Mr. ATKINSON. So I think a couple things.

Your first point about consumers becoming more sophisticated and this in some ways infantilizes them, consumers are becoming more sophisticated, and people know there are bad reviews and good reviews. And so I think as people get more comfortable with the Internet economy, they will be able to sift through that.

In terms of what companies are doing, there are certainly companies, like Yelp and I am sure others, who have very, very sophisticated algorithms. They employ software engineers and data scientists to really be able to use technology to flag these reviews that are at a high risk of being false and then taking them off automatically. So there are companies and there is technology now that companies are employing that, just simply, those reviews don't get posted.

Senator DAINES. Yes, please. Mr. Goldman.

Mr. GOLDMAN. I would like to first point out that no matter how big the problem is with fake reviews, anti-review clauses are never the solution. So this particular bill, I think, is orthogonal to the concern about fake reviews, although I think it is a legitimate concern. But I want to stress how important this bill is, irrespective of whatever concerns anyone has about fake reviews.

But I think with fake reviews we should recognize that consumer reviews are still a relatively new phenomenon. We can take them back maybe as far as 20 years ago, but, really, the modern consumer review economy is maybe a dozen years old.

And if you think about it in those terms, we are seeing the evolution of review sites in developing better and more aggressive techniques for managing consumer reviews. And, in the end, they are the solution. We need to have trustworthy platforms for consumer reviews, and I think that we are seeing improvement on that front every day.

Senator DAINES. You know, I worked for Procter & Gamble before that for 12 years. I mean, this is incredible, valuable data. This is what you used to pay a lot of money to focus groups for. And now we get it virtually real-time, unedited, right at the coalface of the consumer experience.

And that is why I think, yes, these disparagement clauses, I think we are in agreement that we need to deal with that and remove the anti-disparagement clauses based on a lot of stories and Ms. Palmer's story here as well. But this is part of the new economy. This is a gift, I think. If you want to become a world-class company, embrace it.

Mr. Medros?

Mr. MEDROS. Senator Daines, we see over and over again stories like you told. Businesses in remote places and places that consumers wouldn't have thought of traveling to or wouldn't have had the courage to travel to pre-Internet.

And, in fact, the best businesses leverage a platform like TripAdvisor to embrace consumer reviews, to use it as a free marketing tool, to encourage people to share their opinions and set their expectations of what that trip is going to be like so that you feel safe to venture to some of these more remote places that are amazing experiences all around the world. We hear this story over and over again from business owners.

What makes that possible is the scale of our platforms, the free ability for consumers to share those opinions without the threat of being sued or bullied by owners who may not like every piece of feedback.

And the best businesses take that feedback on an ongoing basis and make their business better. They improve their service, they change things about their property, they remodel. They use that as a feedback tool that otherwise companies would have paid millions of dollars for in the past.

Senator DAINES. Thank you.

The CHAIRMAN. Thank you, Senator Daines.

And in our line of work, we get plenty of feedback.

[Laughter.]

Senator DAINES. We do.

The CHAIRMAN. I am really going to embrace the idea that it is a gift.

Senator DAINES. I will stay off of your Facebook; you stay off of mine, Mr. Chairman.

[Laughter.]

The CHAIRMAN. Thank you.

All right. The Senator from Minnesota and noted author, Senator Klobuchar.

STATEMENT OF HON. AMY KLOBUCHAR, U.S. SENATOR FROM MINNESOTA

Senator KLOBUCHAR. Thank you very much, Mr. Chairman.

I was thinking the exact same thing when he said it was a gift. I was thinking of some of the hilarious tweets and Facebook posts that I get. I won't go into them right now, but I collect them because they are so amusing.

So this is a very important bill and subject. And I want to thank the Chairman and Senator Schatz for the work that they have done on this.

And I guess I would start with you, Ms. Palmer. Your experience sounds like quite an ordeal. I read about it. The scale of the harm caused by what was initially a $20 purchase is astounding. And your persistence in finding a solution is extraordinary.

In response to KlearGear's initial demand to take down the review, before they made the negative reports to the credit-rating agencies, how much time would you estimate that you and your husband spent researching and responding to KlearGear's demands?

Ms. PALMER. It was several hours between—I had chosen *RipoffReport.com* seemingly at random. And to find out that they don't allow reviews to come down, it took me several hours to find out what options I had, I believe to the point of actually e-mailing them and saying, "Here is my problem. I am now being bullied. What options do I have?"

And they had to respond to me and kind of spell out and say, "Well, this is in our policy. And the legal language is a little convoluted, but, basically, we don't allow you to take them down, but here is why. We want to make sure that people are free to post a review without feeling bullied and without feeling like they can take it down and without allowing businesses to remove it."

So it was several hours.

Senator KLOBUCHAR. OK.

And, Mr. Rheingold, I think this is kind of one of these softball questions, but do you think most consumers are likely to be as persistent as the Palmers in response to threats from companies seeking to enforce non-disparagement clauses? And what will likely happen if they are not as persistent?

Mr. RHEINGOLD. Ms. Palmer's story is remarkable. I wish all consumers acted like she did. It is really quite amazing. I wish I heard more stories like that. Most people give up. Consumers are not going to pursue their relief. They are going to do whatever they can to just move on with their lives, try to get the review removed.

They, one, as she explained, tried to seek legal help; they couldn't get it. They would just walk away from the problem and probably, unlike Ms. Palmer, stop posting reviews. I think that really would have a chilling effect on most consumers from ever doing it again.

I think, again, Ms. Palmer is unique, and we should clone her in terms of her behavior here.

Senator KLOBUCHAR. Very good. Well, thank you.

I remember I once had a similar thing with a bill, only I had found some people that had pursued things, like Ms. Palmer did, to talk about it. It was about cramming on phone bills. And it was, like, a Lutheran minister and a math teacher had gone to the depth to see these tiny little charges that added up over time.

So you are in good company, I guess.

I understand the concerns of small-business owners who worry that unfair or false reviews can hurt their livelihoods.

Was it you, Mr. Atkinson, who cited a study showing—was it you who had the study showing that a one-star increase in a restaurant's rating on Yelp can lead to a 5- to 9-percent increase in revenue? To put a less rosy spin on it, a one-star decrease in a business's rating can have a serious consequence on its bottom line.

Despite non-disparagement clauses, what tools do you think small-business owners have to address false reviews?

Mr. ATKINSON. Well, first of all, in the lion's share of those ratings, there are accurate reviews. And so the most important thing a restaurant in that particular case could do would be to improve their service or the quality of their food or whatever else they might—why they are getting a bad review. And, again—a couple of people said this—that is valuable information for a company to be able to continuously improve their service.

Second, as I said, a lot of these platforms, including Yelp, TripAdvisor, have mechanisms in place where you can challenge reviews that are bad, not in the sense of taking someone to court, but just say this is a bad review.

Third, companies can and do post and say, "We don't agree with this review, and here is why we don't agree with it," or, "We do agree with this review, and here is why we are sorry, and here is how we are going to fix it."

Senator KLOBUCHAR. I look at a lot of these trips. I was looking at some last night, actually—not in preparation for this hearing, but I would like to say it was—and I have seen those.

And, Mr. Medros, what incentives do you think companies like TripAdvisor have to limit unfair and false reviews?

Mr. MEDROS. We give consumers this ability to share all of their experiences, and the incentive, ultimately, when we hear about limits to free speech, is to warn and then penalize businesses that try to chill that speech.

Senator KLOBUCHAR. Uh-huh.

And, Professor Goldman, does your research bear out what Mr. Medros just talked about?

Mr. GOLDMAN. I am sorry, which aspect?

Senator KLOBUCHAR. Well, he talked about the fact that there are incentives for companies to limit unfair and false reviews.

Mr. GOLDMAN. I am sorry, you are talking about review sites?

Senator KLOBUCHAR. Yes.

Mr. GOLDMAN. Yes. In fact, review sites live and fall on their own reputation. So they are the mechanism for providing that feedback to the marketplace, but they, themselves, compete in the marketplace to be considered to be reputable and persuasive.

And so, in fact, we see fierce competition among review sites to convince their consumers that they are trustworthy. And that competition, actually, is a great incentive to fight against fake reviews.

Senator KLOBUCHAR. All right.

Thank you very much to all of you.

Thank you.

The CHAIRMAN. Thank you, Senator Klobuchar.

Senator Blumenthal?

STATEMENT OF HON. RICHARD BLUMENTHAL, U.S. SENATOR FROM CONNECTICUT

Senator BLUMENTHAL. Thanks, Mr. Chairman.

And I want to thank the Chairman for not only having this hearing but lending his support to the idea of protecting consumers against this new, ingenious wrinkle in the sort of age-old practice of burying tricks and traps in the fine print of contracts. It kind of gives new meaning to hidden tricks and traps that discourage consumers from informing and warning other potential consumers about the downsides of particular experiences of products.

These sorts of sneaky sentences or paragraphs essentially gag a consumer from giving services or goods a negative review when they have paid for it, they are disappointed in it, and they want to warn other consumers.

Usually, they are buried, as you know, in the fine print of a sales contract or an invoice. And they are a one-way ratchet; they prohibit negative reviews but not positive ones. So, from an economic standpoint, they distort the free market and they chill speech.

I am a supporter of the bipartisan bill that has been announced. And I want to thank him for engaging with me on this bill. My initial objection arose from the original language of the bill, which included a provision related to State Attorney General enforcement. That was concerning to me, as a former Attorney General. I believe that the language will be removed when we move to a markup, and so I am proud to add my support as a cosponsor of this bill.

Attorneys General have a vital and vigorous role in protecting consumers and adding to the resources and intellectual weight of the Federal Government. And so I very much appreciate the Chairman's understanding in that regard.

Some probably are going to raise the question, why do we need a Federal law? And the answer is, quite simply, that these standardized anti-defamation provisions may be considered void under State common law, but there are a number of them throughout the country, and they confuse consumers because consumers have to go to different State laws to know whether or not they are valid in one state or another state.

And I would like to simply say that making these provisions a per se violation of the FTC Act is exactly the right thing to do. Prohibiting their use and the chilling effect they create in the first place promotes the free market nationally. And these products, services are sold and marketed nationally, and the information should be available nationally without the impediment of a patchwork of different state laws.

So I would like to ask Mr. Goldman and Mr. Medros, can you talk about the virtue of a Federal solution here? Let's say a Connecticut consumer gets a hotel through a website located in North Dakota for a hotel in Utah. Should a consumer have to research the state laws in three different jurisdictions before she can exercise her free-speech rights?

Mr. MEDROS. Certainly, we would think Ms. Palmer's case is a great example of how difficult it is for a consumer to, one, understand the limits of these clauses and, two, to get relief from them.

They don't add any value to anybody in the ecosystem. They certainly hurt consumers. They probably and certainly hurt other businesses that play by the rules. And they depress the overall market.

Senator BLUMENTHAL. Thank you.

Mr. Goldman?

Mr. GOLDMAN. Yes, I would simply add that, to the extent that we believe that the clauses might already be illegal, that might depend on things like states' interpretations of unconscionability or public policy. And there are significant state and regional variations on those legal doctrines, and, as a result, providing a Federal standard would clean up any ambiguities.

Senator BLUMENTHAL. Thank you.

My time has expired. This subject is one that is extremely important, and I thank you all for being here today.

Thanks, Mr. Chairman.

The CHAIRMAN. Thank you, Senator Blumenthal.

Senator Markey?

STATEMENT OF HON. EDWARD MARKEY, U.S. SENATOR FROM MASSACHUSETTS

Senator MARKEY. Thank you, Mr. Chairman, very much. And thank you for convening today's hearing.

Online review sites provide customers with an important and open forum to provide feedback, to share experiences, and hold businesses accountable. Some of these websites even allow customers to compare products and prices amongst many service providers, helping consumers select the best product at the most affordable price.

Last week, I visited TripAdvisor's headquarters in Needham, Massachusetts, and saw firsthand TripAdvisor's wonderful staff working on key innovations and interfaces needed to ensure consumers have unfettered access to online reviews and travel prices. And I am proud that one of the largest travel sites in the world is based in Massachusetts, and I am happy to see TripAdvisor testifying here today.

It has come to my attention that some airlines may be restricting access to their schedules and prices, making it difficult for online travel sites like TripAdvisor to post different flight options online. If a consumer cannot view all of the flight options and prices on one website, the consumer may be unable to identify the best travel prices. As a result, the consumer may pay too much for their flight.

Mr. Medros, how are consumers harmed when airlines do not provide fare and schedule information to travel sites?

Mr. MEDROS. Consumers are harmed anytime you reduce transparency. In this case, it would be pricing and availability. And given the consolidation in the airline industry, particularly in the

United States, that limit of information, that limit of visibility around real pricing, real availability, real fees, doesn't help consumers plan trips, doesn't help the economy grow through travel and tourism.

Senator MARKEY. Are airlines currently preventing travel sites like TripAdvisor from accessing ticket fees and flight schedules?

Mr. MEDROS. Yes. Increasingly, airlines are attempting to withhold that information and not make it freely available for consumers to price compare and shop.

Senator MARKEY. Should, Mr. Medros, airlines provide travel sites with ancillary fee information, as well? The fee on baggage or advance seat selection fees and all those things, should that also be made available so that the consumer can see what the total charge is going to be to fly?

Mr. MEDROS. Absolutely. I can't think of any consumer that wouldn't want to know outright what to expect in terms of pricing.

Senator MARKEY. So we have gag clauses, provisions buried in contracts that discourage customers from posting negative reviews online, which ultimately may wind up hurting consumers and businesses alike. And I am concerned about these efforts to stifle Americans' freedom to post reviews.

Mr. Medros, as we have learned today, some customers are getting penalized for posting honest but critical reviews, and the mere threat of penalizing customers from posting negative reviews may discourage some customers from posting at all.

Without customers posting their honest assessments of products and services, other customers may not have the information needed to make informed purchasing decisions. How can gag clauses also hurt businesses?

Mr. MEDROS. Gag clauses hurt businesses by reducing the amount of feedback that they get and by distorting the marketplace for other businesses in that market.

Senator MARKEY. OK.

Mr. Rheingold, what other attacks on consumer rights are some businesses including in contracts and terms of service?

Mr. RHEINGOLD. Sure. This is kind of the end of the line. I mean, we have seen it going on for years and years, clauses that restrict people's ability to get into court. Arbitration clauses have been existing for a long time, have now grown to be widespread across every single industry you can imagine, where people who have complaints simply cannot get into our public system of justice. It is a real concern.

And the right to speak is sort of just naturally following the right to go to court. So I am not surprised at all by what we are seeing today.

Senator MARKEY. Thank you.

Ms. Palmer has highlighted one of the more egregious examples of gag clauses. Can you, Mr. Medros, provide other examples of consumers being harassed for posting a negative review?

Mr. MEDROS. Absolutely. We have seen in the past cases, similar gag clauses, with fines upwards of $5 million and daily fines of $50,000 to consumers until the reviews are removed. We have heard of cases from consumers who have contacted us to remove a review because of the threat of a lawsuit or the threat of other action against that individual.

In all of these cases, the consumer stands by their content but is choosing to remove their content and squelch their own speech so as not to end up, in the case of Ms. Palmer, with a lien against them.

Senator MARKEY. OK. Thank you.

Thank you, Mr. Chairman.

The CHAIRMAN. Thank you, Senator Markey.

I just had a couple quick questions here, and we will close this out.

This would be directed to Mr. Atkinson or Professor Goldman. But are there particular industries where consumer gag clauses are especially pervasive?

Mr. GOLDMAN. I mentioned in my initial testimony about the medical and healthcare industry, where the entire industry was encouraged to adopt these restrictions, and many participants—I don't know exactly what percentage, but many participants did so.

I think that that industry has moved on. I would like to think that they have recognized the error of their ways. But I think it is an illustration of how the clauses can sweep an entire industry. Once a few people try it, other businesses might say, "That sounds like a pretty good idea. That gives me the control over my reputation I want. And if I don't do it, other of my competitors are going to be having the glossy reviews while I will have the good and bad aired out in public."

So, in my opening remarks, I did mention that I think that we will see many other industries where the clauses will sweep that are driven by small businesses and professional service providers, so lawyers, doctors, accountants, et cetera, as well as small-business owners. Places like hotels or bed and breakfasts are good, fertile grounds for the breeding of these kinds of clauses.

The CHAIRMAN. OK.

Anything to add to that, Mr. Atkinson?

Mr. ATKINSON. No, I would agree with that. Certainly, health care, retail, hospitality, personal services, companies where you are dealing individually with the actual service provider.

The CHAIRMAN. OK.

And I would direct this to everybody on the panel, but some of you are familiar with the bill that we have introduced, the Consumer Review Freedom Act. And the question I have is, do you believe it strikes an appropriate balance in terms of consumer rights versus the ability of businesses to protect their reputations?

Mr. GOLDMAN. Businesses have already a wide range of tools to protect their reputation. I can't come up with a single circumstance where it is legitimate to tell consumers they can't share their honest, truthful feedback.

So, in my mind, on the particular question that the bill addresses, there is no balance that I can see that would be appropriate to be worried about. It is really, in my mind, an abuse of the business-consumer relationship to tell consumers, "We want your money, but we don't want you talking about it."

The CHAIRMAN. OK.

Anybody else?

Mr. RHEINGOLD. I agree. I mean, I think the bill is a very strong bill and a very important bill, and I think it protects consumers. And I think, as Mr. Goldman said, there are rights that businesses can pursue.

I think it is very strong bill, again. And now that that one provision is being stripped, we are very happy to support it.

OK. Thanks, Mr. Rheingold.

Ms. Palmer?

Ms. PALMER. I would also like to point out that, as consumers, as it has been stated, we don't have a lot of power when it comes to trying to defend ourselves against a business that would seek to have us remove a review or seek to come after us. They have a lot more money. They have a lot more lawyers on staff than we could ever choose to get.

Knowing that there is a law in place that says, ''You guys can't come after us just because we told the truth,'' is extremely empowering to consumers. I believe it will go a long way.

The CHAIRMAN. Thanks.

Mr. Atkinson?

Mr. ATKINSON. I agree with Mr. Goldman; I don't think there is really anything here to balance. What your legislation is trying to prevent are things that are simply unfair and harmful to consumers.

As we have all said, businesses have many other options that this bill would not take away.

The CHAIRMAN. Go ahead.

Mr. MEDROS. I would just add that not only are consumers harmed, but other businesses that play by the rules and want a level playing field are also harmed by the existence of gag clauses that distort the market.

The CHAIRMAN. OK.

Well, thank you all very much. And thank you for your testimony today, for your responses to our questions.

And, Ms. Palmer, thank you for your inspirational story, an example that one person really can make a difference. I think you were sort of the reason why this issue has taken on a life of its own and certainly why we are here today.

And thank you to all the panelists.

You know, we spend a lot of time on this committee, in the Commerce Committee, studying these issues related to the Internet, how do we keep the Internet ecosystem protected, how do we look at the potential that it offers. You look at the digital economy and how powerful that is and how many people are using that to do business, to purchase products and services.

And, obviously, what is happening out there in terms of these various practices seems to completely contradict what we are trying to accomplish, in terms of creating more freedom and protecting consumers' rights out there but certainly empowering people as they use this powerful tool in a way that can enhance not only their lives but those around them as well.

And so we appreciate your insights, and thank you again for making the time to be here today.

We are going to try our best, as we move forward—we have a markup scheduled here in a couple of weeks, and we will hopefully try and move this bill to the Senate floor and try and get some action on it there. We have a companion bill in the House, and it would be nice to see something that we could actually put on the President's desk that would address an issue that I think is becoming increasingly important in our digital economy.

So the hearing record will remain open for two weeks. During this time, Senators will be asked to submit any additional questions for the record. Upon receipt, we would ask the witnesses to submit their written answers to the Committee as soon as possible.

Thank you all again for being here today.

This hearing is adjourned.

[Whereupon, at 11:42 a.m., the hearing was adjourned.]

APPENDIX

Prepared Statement of Scott Michelman, Staff Attorney, Public Citizen

Mr. Chairman Thune, Ranking Member Nelson, and Members of the Committee—

My name is Scott Michelman, and I am a staff attorney at Public Citizen Litigation Group. Public Citizen is a national public interest organization with more than 400,000 members and supporters. For more than 40 years, we have successfully advocated before Congress, the courts, and Federal agencies for stronger measures to protect consumers from unscrupulous business practices. Public Citizen also stands for the free flow of information and ideas, including the rights of consumers to share their opinions and experiences in the marketplace and to learn from the opinions and experiences of others.

In my testimony today, I'll begin by explaining the problem that the Committee has called this hearing to examine: the gagging of consumers who try to write truthful reviews. I'll address the nature of the problem, the harms it causes, and its prevalence. I will then articulate Public Citizen's position: We support congressional action on this issue. Although we cannot support S.B. 2044 in its current form because of a clause that limits its enforcement by state officials, we have been informed by members of the Committee that this clause will be removed. When that change is made, we will strongly support the bill.

The Non-Disparagement Clause and Its Harms

Non-disparagement clauses are terms in consumer contracts—rarely, if ever, negotiated or knowingly agreed to and usually buried in the fine print—that purport to strip the consumer of his or her ability to criticize the company with whom he or she is doing business. Non-disparagement clauses usually specify monetary penalties for violations, penalties that can range from hundreds to thousands of dollars. Sometimes non-disparagement clauses apply specifically to "criticism" or "negative reviews"; in other instances, they prohibit public comment of any type. Sometimes non-disparagement clauses extend beyond reviews to prohibit other actions consumers may wish to take if they feel they are being dealt with unfairly: For instance, some clauses we have seen ban or restrict "disputes," whether brought to a third-party such as a credit-card company or even the company imposing the non-disparagement clause itself. Sometimes non-disparagement clauses include provisions assigning to the company the intellectual property rights to any review the consumer may write, so that the company has the ability to force the consumer to remove any review it doesn't approve. One clause we encountered required the consumer to submit her opinions for "legal review" to the company, which claimed that it could force the consumer to submit to mediation and arbitration at her own expense to obtain the right to complain. Although the specifics can differ, non-disparagement clauses have three essential elements in common: (1) they are imposed by companies in the contract or terms of use as a condition of service or sale; (2) they are rarely if ever up for negotiation and generally do not become known to a consumer until he or she is accused of breaching one and threatened with punitive action unless he or she retracts a review that the companies dislikes; and (3) they prohibit consumers from expressing their honest opinions or experiences with other people or entities.

We believe that these clauses are invalid under the contract law of most if not all states, but there is no precedential case law on the subject, and the possibility of invalidity does not deter companies from enforcing these clauses.

Non-disparagement clauses cause several types of harms to the consumers on whom they are imposed as well as harm to the marketplace as a whole:

(1) *Consumers are disabled from expressing themselves.* Most obviously, non-disparagement clauses prohibit expression and thereby impinge upon a freedom that Americans take as a given in most aspects of their lives: the right to speak freely.

(2) *Consumers are subject to bullying.* The non-disparagement clause gives the business that imposes it huge leverage over the consumer. The clauses are generally legalistic in phrasing and specify a monetary penalty, and companies usually invoke them when they believe consumers have already violated them. As a result, when a company demands that a consumer retract a truthful expression of his or her experience or opinion, the consumer is likely to feel a great deal of pressure to comply with the company's demands. Factors that compound the pressure on consumers include the fact that most Americans are not lawyers and may feel like they do not have the expertise or knowledge to assert their rights, most Americans do not have the ability to hire counsel in these circumstances, companies invoking non-disparagement clauses frequently use intimidating language or threaten that resistance on the part of the consumer will lead to larger monetary penalties either under the terms of the non-disparagement clause or because the consumers will allegedly become liable for attorneys' fees spent to enforce the clause.

(3) *Consumers may be subject to retaliation if they don't retract their reviews.* Threats against consumers may generally be sufficient to achieve a company's ends, but when they are not, consumers may be subject to retaliation. In an extreme case, *Palmer* v. *KlearGear.com,* after online retailer KlearGear demanded $3,500 from Jen and John Palmer for a three-year-old negative online review and they refused to pay, KlearGear falsely reported the money as a "debt" they owed, an action that ruined John Palmer's credit for more than a year and led to numerous denials of credit, accompanied by humiliation, anxiety, and fear. Worst of all, the Palmers could not obtain credit to replace their furnace when it broke and as a result spent weeks' worth of nights, with temperatures around freezing, wrapping their three-year-old son in blankets until they could save up enough money to buy a new furnace with cash.

(4) *Consumers who are the intended audience of reviews suppressed by non-disparagement clauses receive a distorted view of businesses using the clauses.* Today's consumers increasingly rely on online review sites such as Yelp, TripAdvisor, and Angie's List to research businesses before they decide to buy goods or services. When a business succeeds in using a non-disparagement clause to suppress honest negative reviews, the result is that the business appears more attractive and trustworthy than it would if the full range of reviews were available. In this way, non-disparagement clauses harm even consumers who are not subject to them, by limiting the reviews available to all consumers and inhibiting the free exchange of information and opinions among consumers.

(5) *Scrupulous businesses that don't employ non-disparagement clauses are disadvantaged by the skewing of available reviews.* When a company using a non-disparagement clause to suppress critical reviews is successful in improving its overall image, honest businesses that don't try to gag their consumers seem worse by comparison. Thus, the use of non-disparagement clauses warps the marketplace for businesses as well as consumers.

In sum, non-disparagement clauses impose significant harms on consumers, businesses, and the marketplace as a whole, all by inhibiting a core American value: free expression.

Non-Disparagement Clauses Serve No Legitimate Purpose

The obvious reason that a company would use a non-disparagement clause is to artificially enhance its own reputation by silencing its critics. No one argues that this purpose is a legitimate one that deserves consideration or respect.

A defender of non-disparagement clauses might argue instead that they are a reasonable tool for businesses to protect their reputation in the Internet age, because a negative online review can be very detrimental. This rationale is a canard.

First, most online review sites already provide an avenue for businesses to defend their reputation—by responding to the criticism and pointing out, for instance, how the business's practices have changed from what a consumer is criticizing or why a consumer's concern is unreasonable. Many businesses take advantage of these features on sites like Yelp. As Justice Brandeis famously explained in interpreting the First Amendment, "If there be time to expose through discussion the falsehood and fallacies . . . the remedy to be applied is more speech, not enforced silence."[1]

Second and more fundamentally, most criticism is lawful and indeed protected by the First Amendment. The only type of review about which businesses have any le-

---

[1] *Whitney* v. *California,* 274 U.S. 357, 377 (1927) (Brandeis, J., concurring in the judgment).

gitimate ground for complaint is the false and defamatory review—which is unprotected by the First Amendment and which is already subject to a cause of action under ordinary tort law for defamation. Accordingly, non-disparagement clauses are unnecessary to defend against *unlawful* reviews (*i.e.*, defamation) and thus serve only to suppress *lawful* reviews.

The Extent of Non-Disparagement Clauses

Public Citizen has litigated three cases concerning non-disparagement clauses and assisted (in a non-litigation capacity) several other individuals in successfully resisting bullying tactics arising out of non-disparagement clauses. In our work, we have become aware that non-disparagement clauses are used by businesses in a number of industries, including online retail, medical services, hospitality (including hotels and vacation home rentals), wedding services, and more.

The website TechDirt compiled a list of such clauses it found online as of December 2014.[2] That list includes a textbook rental company; a seller of wine storage mechanisms; a tour company; a marketing company; and a collection company. Several more companies appear to have simply copied and pasted the non-disparagement clause used by *KlearGear.com* (described in more detail below). The clauses cited include stated penalties ranging from $2,500 to $100,000 for violations.

Specific examples are useful to show how non-disparagement clauses are used and the various contexts in which they arise:

- In *Palmer* v. *KlearGear.com,* online retailer KlearGear invoked a non-disparagement clause in 2012 to try to fine Utah couple Jen and John Palmer $3,500 for a critical online review posted in 2009. KlearGear's non-disparagement clause, which was not inserted into the company's Terms of Sale and Use until years *after* Jen Palmer posted the review at issue, forbade KlearGear's customers from "taking any action that negatively impacts *KlearGear.com,* its reputation, products, services, management or employees." When the couple wouldn't pay the fine and couldn't remove the posting, KlearGear falsely reported the $3,500 as a "debt" they owed, an action that ruined John Palmer's credit for more than a year and led to numerous denials of credit. On behalf of the Palmers, Public Citizen sued KlearGear in 2013 under the Fair Credit Reporting Act and state tort and contract law. KlearGear never appeared in court to defend itself, and in 2014, we won a default judgment declaring the debt invalid and awarding compensatory and punitive damages to the Palmers.[3]

- In *Lee* v. *Makhnevich,* a New York dentist's service contract provided that each patient gave up the right to criticize the dentist publicly and assigned to the dentist the copyright in anything that the patient may later write about the dentist. When a patient later posted an online review complaining about being overcharged, the dentist sent a "takedown" notice to the review sites, claiming that the posting violated her copyright. The dentist also sent the patient a series of invoices demanding payment of $100 for each day the "copyrighted" complaints continued to appear online. Representing the patient, Public Citizen sued the dentist in 2011. In response, the company that created the dentist's contract recommended that its customers stop using it. After the court denied a motion to dismiss the case, the dentist moved abroad and stopped communicating with her lawyer.[4]

- In *Cox* v. *Accessory Outlet* (later *Cox* v. *Blue Professional*) a Wisconsin consumer who hadn't received her order from an online retailer told the company she was going to contact her credit card company. In response, the company demanded that Cox pay $250 under its fine-print "Terms of Sale," which prohibited "any complaint, chargeback, claim, dispute," the making of "any public statement," or threats to take any of these actions, within 90 days of purchase. The company threatened to report the $250 "debt" to credit reporting agencies, to damage Cox's credit score, and to have a collections agency call Cox's home, cell, and work phones "continuously." The company ominously warned Cox that that it had enforced the terms of sale against "many individuals" and that Cox was "playing games with the wrong people and [had] made a very bad mistake." Public Citizen represented Cox in filing suit in 2014. We discovered that the business that threatened Cox was part of a larger company that did business

---

[2] *See https://www.techdirt.com/articles/20141214/16102629441/here-are-companies-that-want-to-charge-you-2500-100000-negative-reviews.shtml.*

[3] For key case documents, see *http://www.citizen.org/litigation/forms/cases/getlinkforcase.cfm?cID=851.* The case is No. 1:13–cv–00175 (D. Utah).

[4] For key case documents, see *http://www.citizen.org/litigation/forms/cases/getlinkforcase.cfm?cID=706.* The case is No. 11–civ–8665 (S.D.N.Y.).

using four different names and websites, all of which had reportedly engaged in similar practices or imposed similar terms. The company never appeared in court but in response to our lawsuit, all four websites went dark and remain so today. We won a default judgment.[5]

- The Union Street Guest House, a hotel in Hudson, N.Y., included terms in its wedding contracts providing that the wedding couple could be fined if a guest leaves a negative review. After this clause, which apparently had been used to threaten at least one customer, was reported widely in the press in August 2014, the business changed its terms.[6]
- The egg-donor matching site Fertility Bridges, based in Illinois and California, tried to bully a dissatisfied consumer into silence using a non-disparagement clause earlier this year. The company backed down after Public Citizen confronted the company with the ambiguous language of its clause and its illegality under applicable California law.[7]

Public Citizen has received several other complaints concerning non-disparagement clauses, the details of which cannot be disclosed on account of attorney-client privilege.

To date, only one jurisdiction, California, has banned non-disparagement clauses.[8]

Just as troubling as the cases we know about are the instances we don't know about—instance in which a consumer does not contact a lawyer but instead backs down and retracts a critical review in the face of a business's threats. Given the aggressive behavior in the instances documented above, along with the high fines companies seek to enforce and the fact that companies are asserting consumers are already in the wrong when the companies demand retractions, most people likely feel strong pressure to cooperate and therefore understandably acquiesce to a business's demands. Accordingly, the harm from non-disparagement clauses almost certainly extends beyond the instances we know about.

Current legal tools are insufficient to address the problem of non-disparagement clauses because many consumers do not have the resources to hire a lawyer and do not feel empowered to assert their rights in the face of bullying tactics and legalistic language. Additionally, as illustrated by the websites that have copied KlearGear's non-disparagement clause, KlearGear's loss in court has not prevented other businesses from following its model. And KlearGear itself continues to evade efforts to collect on the judgment against it. Legislation and robust enforcement by Federal and state authorities are likely to be the most powerful weapons against non-disparagement clauses.

Public Citizen's Position on S.B. 2044

Public Citizen strongly supports a legislative response to the problem of non-disparagement clauses. As explained below, we cannot support S.B. 2044 in its current form, but we understand that there is an agreement to amend it to a version we would support, and we look forward to supporting it after amendment.

S.B. 2044 rightly bans non-disparagement clauses and provides for both Federal and state enforcement of this new prohibition. However, Section 2(e)(7) of the proposed bill needlessly hinders state enforcement by barring state attorneys general from working with outside counsel on a contingency fee basis.

Government enforcement is vital to the enforcement of consumer protection laws. Many state enforcement offices are under-resourced and are unlikely to enforce these laws if they cannot do it in partnership with outside counsel. Public Citizen therefore categorically opposes any provisions barring states from hiring outside counsel for enforcement purposes because such provisions serve no purpose but to weaken enforcement. Additionally, states hire outside counsel all the time for all kinds of legal work. Carving out consumer protection measures for special restrictions on outside enforcement consigns these important laws to a second-class status in terms of states' ability to enforce them.

Specific to the context of non-disparagement clauses, effective enforcement against the types of companies using these provisions can be difficult; in all three cases Public Citizen has brought to court, we have encountered problems with defendants fleeing abroad or hiding their assets. Bringing in private counsel might be the best

---

[5] For key case documents, see *http://www.citizen.org/litigation/forms/cases/getlinkforcase.cfm?cID=893*. The case is No. 652643/2014 (N.Y. Sup. Ct.).

[6] See *http://pubcit.typepad.com/clpblog/2014/08/internet-shames-new-york-hotel-into-removing-non-disparagement-clause-fining-wedding-couple-for-thei.html*.

[7] See *http://pubcit.typepad.com/clpblog/2015/10/fertility-bridges-use-of-a-nondisparagement-clause-to-bully-dissatisfied-customers.html*.

[8] *See* Cal. Civil Code 1670.8.

way to enforce the ban on non-disparagement clauses without unduly detracting from states' other important law enforcement work.

For these reasons, we cannot support the bill in its current form, but we are pleased to have learned that the Committee has agreed to remove Section 2(e)(7), and we look forward to supporting the bill once that has occurred.

Conclusion

Non-disparagement clauses harm consumers, honest businesses, and the marketplace in general. They lead to the bullying of consumers and the chilling or suppression of speech on which consumers rely to make informed decisions in the marketplace. In recent years, non-disparagement clauses have appeared in a variety of contexts. Litigation under current laws is insufficient to address the problem.

Public Citizen therefore believes that congressional action is needed to address the significant problem of non-disparagement clauses. We cannot support S.B. 2044 in its current form because of the restriction on state enforcement contained in Section 2(e)(7), but once that provision is removed, we will strongly support the bill.

I thank you for the opportunity to address the Committee.

PREPARED STATEMENT OF ANGIE HICKS, FOUNDER AND CHIEF MARKETING OFFICER, ANGIE'S LIST

Senator Thune,

Thank you for the opportunity to speak out strongly in favor of this legislation. Thank you and Sens. Moran and Schatz for bringing this important matter to the Nation's attention. I am sorry that other obligations kept me from addressing you in person about this important legislation but I welcome continued discussion about this matter in the weeks and months ahead.

On behalf of our member and all consumers, I have been speaking in opposition to efforts to stifle honest expression since we discovered in 2009 that some within the medical community were inserting "Mutual Agreement to Maintain Privacy" forms within their patient paperwork.

I am proud that Angie's List was one of the first to speak out against this practice and helped end the trend in the health care arena. When we learned about the agreements, the company pushing them had already signed up 2,000 physicians.

I started speaking out about it to the national news media—TV news shows, newspapers, online publications—any outlet that would help us raise awareness. I wrote repeatedly about it on my blog, and warned our members through our magazine, e-mails and alerts on company profiles.

Not long after we started speaking out, the company selling the agreements to physicians reached out to me personally to try to convince me the agreements were a good step forward. Suffice it to say I was not convinced. Not long after that, the company stopped selling the agreements.

Unfortunately, since then, other similar efforts have erupted in other types of business. The latest efforts are "non-disparagement clauses" within service contracts, which businesses use to threaten legal action against their own customers simply for speaking their mind.

The bipartisan Consumer Review Freedom Act would prohibit the use of these clauses, agreements and waivers, which are blatant—though often cleverly disguised—efforts to strip Americans of their right to honestly discuss their service experience.

Angie's List has collected and shared consumer reviews for 20 years in an effort to help consumers find reliable, high quality service companies and just recently accepted our 10 millionth verified review. We have never accepted anonymous reviews and we require members to affirm they are giving us their honest feedback on their own experience.

I could spend hours telling you of the companies that have been able to grow from literally "a guy in a truck" to thriving businesses, including franchises across the country because they have earned high grades from Angie's List members.

I could give you dozens of examples of companies that earned negative reviews from Angie's List members, took that criticism to heart, made the members whole and turned their businesses around thanks to the customer insight.

A common argument for using gag orders is that they protect companies from untrue and/or anonymous criticism. At Angie's List, our members reaffirm they are giving honest feedback about their own experience each time they submit a review. If reviews—on our site or any other—are untrue or malicious, there are already legal remedies at hand under existing libel and defamation laws.

I don't think you need me to tell you that stifling consumer expression is simply wrong. There is no benefit or need for these gag orders whatsoever.

As a consumer advocate, Angie's List can only go so far to stop this kind of unwarranted, right-stifling tactics. But you, the Congress, can outlaw these practices.

I urge you to use your power, pass this legislation and stand up for consumers.

CONSUMERS UNION
November 3, 2015

Hon. JOHN THUNE,
Chairman,
Hon. BILL NELSON,
Ranking Member,
Committee on Commerce, Science, and Transportation,
United States Senate,
Washington, DC.

Dear Chairman Thune and Ranking Member Nelson:

Consumers Union, the policy and advocacy arm of *Consumer Reports,* is pleased that your Committee is holding hearings on the troubling use of non-disparagement clauses, or "consumer gag clauses," in standard-form consumer contracts. S. 2044, the Consumer Review Freedom Act, would help protect consumers' freedom of speech in the marketplace, by making it illegal for businesses to stop their customers from writing negative online reviews, or to punish their customers for doing so.

Today, consumers regularly offer their personal reviews about hotels, restaurants, and other products and services online. Unfortunately, some businesses have sought to block consumers from communicating such information to each other—by taking them to court, or by threatening to. Some businesses have inserted "non-disparagement clauses" into the lengthy boilerplate in their standard-form consumer purchase agreements. These paragraphs purport to indicate that the consumer has supposedly agreed to waive the right to say anything negative about the product or service or business. Or that the consumer has supposedly turned over to the business a copyright ownership for any review the consumer might write, so that the business can stop the review from being published or can threaten suit for copyright infringement. At least one business reportedly tried to use a consumer's supposed liability under a non-disparagement clause to ruin the consumer's personal credit rating.

These same tactics could also potentially be used against professional product and service testers and raters. At *Consumer Reports,* for example, we buy the products and services we test and rate in the marketplace, anonymously. Indeed, it is a hallmark of the integrity and credibility of our ratings that sellers do not know they are selling their product or service to *Consumer Reports*—that by outward appearances, we are an individual buying for personal use.

Consumer Reports is also a forum for the views of individual consumers. We survey consumers regarding their experiences in various product and service sectors, and publish the results. Sometimes we report an individual consumer's experience. A consumer's participation in these activities could also be attacked as an alleged violation of a non-disparagement clause.

It is no exaggeration to say that non-disparagement clauses in consumer purchase agreements could be exploited to interfere with our ability at *Consumer Reports* to bring objective, unbiased, reliable information to the consuming public about the safety and performance of products and services—and more broadly, could be exploited in an attempt to silence the consumer voice.

S. 2044 would help stop these outrageous anti-consumer tactics, by making such non-disparagement clauses in consumer contracts null and void. And it would give the Federal Trade Commission and state attorneys general authority to turn the tables and take enforcement action against businesses that attempt to use these clauses against consumers.

Consumers Union looks forward to working with you to enact effective legislation to protect the rights of consumers to speak their honest opinion about the products and services they purchase, and about how they are treated by the businesses they deal with.

Thank you for your leadership on this important consumer rights issue.
　　Sincerely,

GEORGE P. SLOVER,
Senior Policy Counsel,
Consumers Union.

cc: Members, Senate Committee on Commerce, Science, and Transportation

---

R STREET INSTITUTE, INSTITUTE FOR LIBERTY
AMERICAN CONSUMER INSTITUTE
November 4, 2015

Hon. JOHN THUNE,
Hon. BILL NELSON,
United States Senate,
Committee on Commerce, Science, and Transportation,
Washington, DC.

FREE-MARKET, TAXPAYER, AND CONSUMER GROUPS SUPPORT THE CONSUMER REVIEW FREEDOM ACT

Dear Committee Members,

As free-market organizations, we write to express our strong support for your committee's ongoing efforts to defend commerce and freedom of expression. In particular, as advocates for a free and open Internet that facilitates robust online markets, we urge you to support the critical free-speech protections in the Consumer Review Freedom Act of 2015 (S. 2044).

We take this position for one simple reason: when conducting business on the Internet, firms must maintain good reputations to stay competitive. Without this channel for accountability and transparency, public confidence in online commerce itself would be undermined.

The Internet is a critical nexus for commerce, providing a quarter-billion Americans with access to new markets and enhanced economic opportunities. Of central importance to these online markets is their ability to conduct reliable transactions with a full range of commercial firms and entrepreneurial individuals.

Thanks to online reviews and feedback, consumers can feel secure doing business with those whom they've never met to make a purchase, get a ride, arrange a place to stay or conduct myriad other transactions. Potential customers also have access to far better, richer information about restaurants, hotels and local service providers than ever before. Online reviews are an essential channel for reputational feedback; they provide online firms and entrepreneurs with the greatest incentives to maximize benefits to customers.

Unfortunately, bad actors sometimes use abusive lawsuits to silence their critics and weaken their competitors. This undermines everyone's ability to engage in an open, transparent and free market.

The Consumer Review Freedom Act addresses this issue by targeting non-disparagement clauses, which sometimes are buried within firms' terms of service or other non-negotiable agreements and which restrict consumers' ability to review their experiences fairly and honestly. These agreements represent unfair contracts of adhesion and threaten to strangle the vast economic benefits of online reviews. Furthermore, they restrict freedom of speech and undermine the promise and spirit of the First Amendment.

We urge you to support this package of reforms to help create a strong national standard for the protection of both free expression and free markets.
　　Sincerely,

MIKE GODWIN,
R Street Institute.
MYTHEOS HOLT,
Institute for Liberty.
STEVE POCIASK,
American Consumer Institute.

INTERNET ASSOCIATION
Washington, DC, November 4, 2015

Hon. JOHN THUNE,
Chairman,
Senate Committee on Commerce,
Science, and Transportation,
United States Senate,
Washington, DC.

Hon. BILL NELSON,
Ranking Member,
Senate Committee on Commerce,
Science, and Transportation,
United States Senate,
Washington, DC.

Dear Chairman Thune and Ranking Member Nelson:

The Internet Association is the unified voice of the Internet economy, representing the interests of leading Internet companies and their global community of users.[1] It is dedicated to advancing public policy solutions to strengthen and protect Internet freedom, foster innovation and economic growth, and empower users. Important to our mission is the advancement of public policies that preserve free speech online. We applaud today's hearing on *The Consumer Review Freedom Act* (S. 2044), a bipartisan bill introduced by Chairman Thune, Senator Schatz, and Senator Jerry Moran.[2]

In today's digital economy, nearly 70 percent of consumers now rely on online consumer reviews for information on where to eat, shop, travel, and more.[3] The Internet enables millions of consumers to access timely, honest feedback that empowers them to make informed choices when purchasing goods or services. The result of the efficiency gains for these and other web enabled information sharing is a significant consumer surplus that benefits our economy in myriad ways. Experts calculate this consumer surplus was the equivalent of billions of dollars annually.[4]

Unfortunately, an increasing number of companies who are unhappy with consumer reviews are utilizing non-disparagement clauses, often buried in non-negotiable form contracts, to stifle online consumer free speech. These clauses often impose penalties as high as hundreds of thousands of dollars for negative reviews by unknowing consumers of goods and services nationwide. In particularly egregious cases, individuals have been threatened with reporting to credit agencies and other tactics meant to intimidate and silence consumers.[5]

The range of form contracts engaging in this attempt to stifle speech is varied across the Nation and includes hotels and restaurants, apartment buildings, repair services, and more.[6] As Internet platforms utilized by millions of businesses provide consumers unprecedented opportunities to engage in the feedback economy, the threat against consumer-generated speech is growing rapidly and increasingly difficult to quantify.

A patchwork of state laws, court decisions, and Federal agency actions have attempted to protect consumers subject to non-disparagement clauses. However, we must address the issue on a national level to ensure the protection of all consumers online. The right to free speech—including online reviews and comments from customers—is critical to our rights as Americans and should not be curtailed.

The Consumer Review Freedom Act, which would prohibit the use of these non-defamation clauses, will protect consumers nationwide from these meritless attempts to silence free speech. The Internet Association strongly supports this legislation's effort to protect online reviewers of goods and services from clauses that inhibit honest reviews and commends the Committee for examining this issue in detail during today's hearing.

The Consumer Review Freedom Act is narrowly tailored to non-disparagement clauses in form contracts that do not allow individuals a meaningful chance to negotiate a contract, and provides the necessary protections for businesses, including for

---

[1] The Internet Association's members include Airbnb, Amazon.com, auction.com, Coinbase, Dropbox, eBay, Etsy, Expedia, Facebook, Gilt, Google, Handy, LinkedIn, Lyft, Monster Worldwide, Netflix, Pandora, PayPal, Practice Fusion, Rackspace, reddit, Salesforce.com, Sidecar, Snapchat, SurveyMonkey, TripAdvisor, Twitter, Yahoo, Yelp, Uber, Zenefits, and Zynga.

[2] We respectfully request that this letter be submitted to the record for this hearing.

[3] *American Lifestyles 2015: The Connected Consumer—Seeking Validation from the Online Collective—US 2015*, Mintel (June 3, 2015) *http://www.mintel.com/press-centre/social-and-lifestyle/seven-in-10-americans-seek-out-opinions-before-making-purchases*.

[4] Hal Varian, The value of the Internet now and in the future, The Economist (Mar. 10, 2013, 3:49PM),*http://www.economist.com/blogs/freeexchange/2013/03/technology-1*; Shane Greenstein, Measuring consumer surplus online, The Economist (Mar. 11, 2013, 3:20PM), *http://www.economist.com/blogs/freeexchange/2013/03/technology-2*.

[5] *Palmer v. KlearGear*, No. 13-cv-00175 (D. Utah, filed Dec. 18, 2013).

[6] Tim Cushing, *Here are the Companies that Want to Charge You $2,500–$100,000 for Negative Reviews*, TechDirt (Dec. 17, 2014, 8:27AM), *https://www.techdirt.com/articles/20141214/16102 629441/here-are-companies-that-want-to-charge-you-2500-100000-negative-reviews.shtml*.

medical and personal information, trade secrets, and confidential information.[7] The bill strikes a fair balance between speech rights and legitimate business needs. The Internet Association additionally supports the intent of the bill to combat these clauses in the cases of form contracts for goods and services, and would support clarifying language to provide businesses and agencies certainty in enforcement of this legislation.

We look forward to hearing the discussion at the Committee's hearing today, and to working with you and your staff to pass *The Consumer Review Freedom Act.*

Respectfully submitted,

MICHAEL BECKERMAN,
President and CEO,
The Internet Association.

November 3, 2015

Dear Chairman Thune and Ranking Member Nelson:

Every day, countless Americans use consumer review sites to share their experiences and opinions on the businesses and services they rely upon. These reviews have become instrumental in educating customers and informing their choices on everything from what doctor or mechanic to visit to where to shop, eat, and stay. In fact, today, nearly 70 percent of customers rely on online reviews before making a purchase.[1]

However, companies are now increasingly using unfair non-defamation clauses to silence consumers and limit their right to free speech. Businesses are employing these clauses, which are often hidden in non-negotiable form contracts for goods and services, in order to penalize or monetarily fine customers who decide to share their negative experiences with others in the form of online reviews.

Non-defamation clauses stifle free speech and harm citizens' ability to make informed purchasing decisions, while rewarding bad businesses that are willing to bully their clientele into silence. In response, we are joining together to express our support for the Consumer Review Freedom Act (S. 2044), which we believe will go a long way to protect consumers' right to share legitimate speech on and offline.

This bipartisan legislation, introduced by Sen. John Thune (R–SD), Sen. Brian Schatz (D–HI) and Sen. Jerry Moran (R–KS), strengthens First Amendment protections by prohibiting businesses from using non-defamation clauses to intimidate and muzzle honest reviewers. The Consumer Review Freedom Act will outlaw non-disparagement clauses in consumer contracts nationwide, while protecting the rights of consumers to freely share their experiences and opinions on the Internet without fear of intimidation.

Currently, Americans rely on a patchwork of state laws that do not equally protect the free speech rights of all Americans. Having Federal legislation in place to help preserve the free speech rights of American consumers will go a long way to ensuring deep-pocketed bullies are unable to quiet their critics.

By sharing honest reviews about the places we eat, shop, visit and stay, consumers are using their personal experiences to help their friends and neighbors make informed purchasing decisions while ensuring American businesses are held accountable to their customers. We look forward to working with the Commerce Committee to quickly address any necessary technical amendments that might be needed as the bill moves forward, but wholeheartedly support the Senate's efforts

---

[7] S. 2044, 114th Cong. §2(a)(3) (2015).
[1] The Consumerist (Jun. 3, 2015), *http://consumerist.com/2015/06/03/nearly-70-of-consumers-rely-on-online-reviews-before-making-a-purchase/;* Ashlee Kieler, *Nearly 70% Of Consumers Rely On Online Reviews Before Making A Purchase.*

to pass this important legislation that protects the Internet as an open speech platform.

Respectfully,

———

November 3, 2015

Dear Senator:

On behalf of its low-income clients, the National Consumer Law Center writes in support of the Consumer Review Freedom Act of 2015, S. 2044. This bill would prohibit companies from using non-disparagement clauses in boilerplate, consumer form contracts. While we have objections to the provision limiting the ability of state attorneys general to use contingency fee arrangements when engaging outside counsel, we understand that this provision will be removed during the Committee markup.

We support S.2044 because it protects the rights of consumers to express their opinions in reviewing products and services, especially in online forums. Such reviews help inform other consumers and enable them to comparison shop. Unfortunately, some companies have attempted to suppress or muzzle negative reviews by including contract provisions that restrict consumers' ability to write such reviews. The most notable example was the case of KlearGear, which tried to impose a $3,500 penalty on two consumers for a negative review, even going so far as to report this penalty on their credit reports. S.2044 would prevent such attempts to suppress consumers' ability to freely review products and services.

Please contact me at *cwu@nclc.org* or 617–542–8010 with any questions about this letter.

Sincerely,

CHI CHI WU,
National Consumer Law Center
(on behalf of its low-income clients).

Æ

This page intentionally left blank.

This page intentionally left blank.

This page intentionally left blank.

www.ingramcontent.com/pod-product-compliance
Lightning Source LLC
Chambersburg PA
CBHW080723190526

45169CB00006B/2494